Praise
High-Functioning Anxiety

'Award-winning psychologist Dr. Lalitaa takes us on a transformative
journey offering practical solutions and insightful reflections, empowering
readers to confront anxiety through a psychology-based approach. A
must-read lifeline, it instills the belief that inner peace is within reach.'

VEX KING, *SUNDAY TIMES* BEST-SELLING AUTHOR OF
GOOD VIBES, GOOD LIFE

'Break free from high-functioning anxiety with this
ultimate guide to thrive, not just survive!'

SHIVANI PAU, HOST OF *THE MILLENNIAL MIND* PODCAST

'This book is a transformative guide to embracing self-worth and
overcoming high-functioning anxiety, offering practical tools and profound
insights to help you accept your authentic self and thrive beyond boundaries.'

SIMRAN KAUR, AUTHOR OF *GIRLS THAT INVEST*

'Dr. Lalitaa helps you understand what it is you've been feeling
and then tells you what you should do with it. Fascinating.'

MO GAWDAT, ENTREPRENEUR AND BEST-SELLING AUTHOR

'*High-Functioning Anxiety* is an impactful read for anyone that has
mastered the act of appearing "fine" on the outside, but is inwardly
struggling with self-doubt, fear of failure, or perfectionism. Dr. Lalitaa
combines her lived experience with expert knowledge to provide readers
with a supportive road map toward self-discovery and growth.'

MEREDITH CARDER, ADHD COACH AND AUTHOR OF
IT ALL MAKES SENSE NOW

'Rich with case studies, practical advice, and professional and personal wisdom, this book offers solutions for those suffering the confusion of being unknowingly anxious and high-functioning. A must-read on the journey to healing.'

SIMONE HENG, AUTHOR OF *LET'S TALK ABOUT LONELINESS*

'I value giving people tools and frameworks for them to work through their issues rather than having the reader intellectualize their issues and stay in the same cycles. Dr. Lalitaa's *High-Functioning Anxiety* artfully provides not just the information and context but also gives you the tools to work through issues as they arise. The practical exercises and self-reflection questions provided are transformative for individuals stuck in consistent patterns. I have been a fan of Lalitaa's work (and her as a person) for many years, and *High-Functioning Anxiety* might just be her best work to date.'

SABRINA ZOHAR, HOST OF *DO THE WORK* PODCAST

'High-functioning anxiety often results in us hiding from ourselves and avoiding the pain that is driving us, which leads to further suffering in the form of isolation and loneliness. Dr. Lalitaa's book is so special because she will help you feel less alone. In her warm and empathetic style, she will be your guide to more deeply understanding the history that has led you to this place, and then will hold your hand through a proven path to healing. I highly recommend this important book.'

ALEX HOWARD, FOUNDER OF THE OPTIMUM HEALTH CLINIC AND AUTHOR OF *IT'S NOT YOUR FAULT*

'This feels like a book for our time. At its root, it's an invitation – from somebody with powerful lived and learned experience – to live beyond the confines of the mind's often fear-driven chatter, and break cycles. While Dr. Lalitaa has created the book for those who identify as having high-functioning anxiety, many more people are living with heightened levels of anxiety post pandemic – I've no doubt this book will be a huge support in the journey to unlearning and relearning for so many.'

JESSICA HUIE, AUTHOR OF *PURPOSE*

high function -ing anxiety

Dr. Lalitaa
Suglani

high

function

-ing

A 5-step guide
to calming
the inner panic
and thriving

anxiety

HAY HOUSE

Carlsbad, California • New York City
London • Sydney • New Delhi

Published in the United Kingdom by:
Hay House UK Ltd, The Sixth Floor, Watson House
54 Baker Street, London W1U 7BU
Tel: +44 (0)20 3927 7290; www.hayhouse.co.uk

Published in the United States of America by:
Hay House LLC, PO Box 5100, Carlsbad, CA 92018-5100
Tel: (1) 760 431 7695 or (800) 654 5126; www.hayhouse.com

Published in Australia by:
Hay House Australia Publishing Pty Ltd, 18/36 Ralph St, Alexandria NSW 2015
Tel: (61) 2 9669 4299; www.hayhouse.com.au

Published in India by:
Hay House Publishers (India) Pvt Ltd, Muskaan Complex,
Plot No.3, B-2, Vasant Kunj, New Delhi 110 070
Tel: (91) 11 4176 1620; www.hayhouse.co.in

A catalogue record for this book is available from the British Library.

Tradepaper ISBN: 978-1-4019-7660-6
E-book ISBN: 978-1-83782-227-0
Audiobook ISBN: 978-1-83782-226-3

10 9 8 7 6 5 4 3 2 1

Printed in the United States of America

This product uses responsibly sourced papers and/or recycled materials.
For more information, see www.hayhouse.com.

Healing is an act of forgiveness and responsibility between light and shadow. A rebirth mark where we put the pieces together to become whole.

Contents

Introduction

I still remember the moment I chose to finally face my shadows. Growing up as a second-generation British immigrant and ethnic minority, I'd found myself split between two cultures. This shaped my life experience and in an effort to cope, I developed high-functioning anxiety. By the time I reached adulthood, I was filled with shame, and the mental box I was trying to hide it in was running out of space.

I believed that there was something deeply wrong with me, and as my inner critic became louder, I struggled to even look at myself in the mirror. This was my approach to dealing with the way I felt, and only now can I see how unhealthy it was. At the time, I didn't know what was happening to me: I just thought I was stupid and pathetic. I didn't want anyone else to see that, though, so I did whatever I could to ensure this side of me remained hidden.

My 'solution' to my problems was to try and become 'successful,' but at the heart of them lay a lack of values and meaningful connections with others. And although I felt exhausted by it all, I believed there was nothing else I could do. I was scared to ask for help because I didn't want to reveal how 'messed up' I thought

I was. For years, I fought to avoid certain parts of myself, but no matter what I did, they always found a way to emerge. In the end, I had no choice but to force them out of the darkness and into the light. And what I discovered there changed my life.

What Is High-Functioning Anxiety (HFA)?

Before we begin, I want to be clear that high-functioning anxiety – or HFA, as I will refer to it in this book – is not the same as debilitating anxiety, which is generally defined as anxiety that's severe enough to shut us down to the point where we're no longer capable of working, looking after ourselves, or maintaining relationships. People with HFA, people like me, experience the symptoms of their anxiety internally, while still managing their external life effectively. We show the world what we think of as our 'good' side and keep our 'real' side – the anxious one that we don't want others to see – hidden.

According to the USA's National Health Institute of Mental Health, an estimated 31 percent of adults experience an anxiety disorder at some time in their lives,[1] while in the UK, in 2022/23, an average of 37 percent of women and 30 percent of men reported high levels of anxiety.[2]

Now, it's likely that a sizeable proportion of these people with an anxiety disorder suffer with high-functioning anxiety, but despite this, HFA is not currently a recognized anxiety disorder. While it's argued that this is because sufferers tend to function reasonably well in their daily lives, the effects of HFA can be extreme, affecting quality of life and causing intense feelings of loneliness and disconnection.

HFA is rooted in feelings of not being 'good enough.' People with HFA often appear competent and accomplished, but internally, they experience intense worry, self-doubt, and fear of failure. As a result, they often hold themselves to incredibly high standards and constantly strive for perfection in various aspects of their lives. We're often the ones who show up to get things done and make sure everyone else is okay. We look as if we have it all together and are strong and organized, but on the inside it's a different story –one that no one else gets to see.

This fear of not being good enough can drive those of us with HFA to overachieve and excel in a bid to prove our worth via external validation. We fear judgment, and resist saying no to others or letting them down; we may think this is the only way to be accepted and loved by others. However, despite our achievements, we may still feel inadequate and harbor an underlying sense that we don't measure up. Or believe, deep down, that there's something wrong with us. This fear of not being good enough can become a constant source of stress and anxiety and lead to a behavior pattern of overworking, overthinking, and self-criticism.

As a psychologist, one of the interesting, yet perplexing, things I've found is that, while many of the people I meet can relate to the *concept* of high-functioning anxiety, they don't fully understand its underlying *causes*. In fact, they often insist that they *do* feel sufficiently worthy in their lives.

However, it's crucial to understand that, while you may consider yourself to be a confident and contented adult, it doesn't necessarily mean that your actions are free from fear-based motivations – you just might not be able to see it. Often, core issues remain hidden deep in our subconscious while we just scratch at the surface of our self-awareness. It's my intention in this book to help you dig deeper, into your innermost roots, to discover and embrace your authentic self.

Right now, you might be thinking, *Why explore all this if I'm happy the way I am?* My answer: because HFA stops us from truly living life to the full. It limits us and makes us play safe, hiding parts of ourselves from the world. HFA is rooted in *fear*: the fear of other people seeing the 'real' us – yet our internal battle is with ourselves, not others.

Eventually, we reach a point where we become fed up with living in a constant state of hidden anxiety – I can tell you from my own experience that it's a lonely and exhausting place to be. We realize that we have no option other than to look at the *cause* of our anxiety – and we find that the cause is the very thing we've been running away from.

Embracing Our Worthiness

Acknowledging that something's wrong is often the hardest part. The only way to move forward is to be honest with yourself – not to run away or hide behind emotional shields. The process might seem daunting, but it's better than the alternative of living with anxiety. It's time to take personal responsibility and grow into your authentic self.

Just as rain cleanses the earth and gives rise to new growth, the challenges you face have the power to cleanse your spirit and illuminate your path. Within the darkness lies the opportunity for growth and transformation. The storms may shake you, but they're also sculpting the person you're meant to become. Trust in the process for, when the storms subside, you'll stand stronger, wiser, and more aligned with your true self.

This isn't easy, of course. You must do the 'work,' which involves being honest about yourself and your feelings. There's no quick-fix solution; this is a lifestyle change. But trust me, it's worth it. Just as the caterpillar waits in its cocoon, going through different stages of metamorphosis, so too will you spend time within yourself, going deep as you prepare for change. I want people to feel *worthy enough*, and to stop struggling with their thoughts. I've seen this process in action with the people I work with – marveling at how, once they truly *understand* their thoughts, *everything* can change. The journey of life isn't one where we perform for others but one where we love ourselves with compassion and are able to simply 'be.'

We often find ourselves caught in the trap of feeling inadequate or not measuring up to certain standards. However, the truth is that we are *inherently* good enough, just as we are. Our worthiness doesn't depend on external achievements, validations, or comparisons to others. We possess unique qualities, strengths, and gifts that make us valuable and worthy of love and acceptance.

How This Book Works

Embracing our worthiness allows us to cultivate self-compassion, self-acceptance, and inner peace. By recognizing our innate goodness, we can let go of the need for constant striving and perfectionism and instead, accept our authentic self with kindness and love. Reaching the point where you can see that you're *already* enough, simply by being you, is where it all changes.

This is why I've written this book – to give you the awareness, the understanding, and the tools you need to quieten the inner panic of high-functioning anxiety, find balance, and thrive. I'll explain exactly what HFA is and show you how to recognize its symptoms and behavior patterns in your own life. And then I'll help you to adopt a *new* way of being.

With my proven, psychology-based approach – which includes practical exercises and tools, and questions designed for self-reflection – you'll reach for your inner strength and resilience to confront your fears and overcome your anxiety. You *can* accomplish this – it's within your reach, and you deserve it. Get ready to expand and stretch yourself beyond your existing boundaries.

Introducing the Five Steps

This book is a five-step guide to managing HFA organized into two parts. Part I, *Unlearning*, is Steps 1 and 2. When I take clients through the process of overcoming their HFA, the first thing I do is help them to recognize that they *do* have it and then to understand *why* they have it. Without this understanding, we're just managing the symptoms rather than addressing the underlying cause – which is fear. The *unlearning* part comes from reconnecting with ourselves and finding out where that fear originates, and then unlearning the behavior that results from it.

Part II, *Learning*, is Steps 3 to 5, and shows you how to reconnect with yourself. In it, you'll learn how to navigate the heightened sensitivity that's associated with HFA, as well as trust yourself and show yourself compassion. Here's an overview of the five steps:

Step 1: Discover Your Patterns and Unveil Your Hidden Self – This in-depth exploration of HFA sets out what it is and where it comes from, and reveals the ways it manifests in key behavior patterns.

Step 2: Decode Your Patterns, Uncover Your Beliefs, and Face Your Shadow – Dig deeper to identify these behavior patterns in yourself, uncover their origins, and understand why you live the way you do.

Step 3: Develop Self-Connection and Transcend Your Fear – Among other things, this features a comprehensive tool kit to help you manage your fear, anxiety, and self-doubt.

Step 4: Embrace Your Sensitivity and Reclaim Self-Trust – Find out how to set healthy boundaries that will protect you while you're navigating the heightened sensitivity of HFA.

Step 5: Unleash Self-Compassion – Learn the art of being kind to yourself and discover ways to thrive with the help of the 12 'powers.'

Throughout the book, I'll draw on my own experience of HFA, as well as the wisdom I've gained through working with clients in the therapy room over the years; in fact, I've included many client case studies as examples of HFA behavior (note that names and stories have been changed to maintain confidentiality). You'll learn how to face your past, understand the ways that it impacts your present, and create a more fulfilling and meaningful future.

I'm lucky; I eventually found a therapist who created a safe space in which I could confront my shadows and my anxiety. I can still recall how it felt when I started to understand my behavior patterns and things finally began to make sense. I began truly opening my heart and trusting myself in life, and the feeling was beautiful. I felt at peace. Even on the occasions when I faltered, I understood *why* it was happening. It was the start of my journey. Picking up this book is the start of yours.

Unlearn
-ing

STEP 1

Discover Your Patterns and Unveil Your Hidden Self

How often do you not only *say* to yourself things like 'I'm not good enough,' 'I'm such an idiot,' or 'I'm pathetic,' but also *show* it via self-defeating behaviors, attitudes, and self-sabotage? Do you hold a deep belief that there's something's wrong with you, although you're not sure exactly what it is? And does this pattern of behavior repeat itself endlessly, making you feel worse about yourself each time?

Before I went into therapy, I lived *my* life without realizing I was caught up in this behavioral rut. I'd always been the strong one – caring about everyone else, putting their needs first, and showing up as the person who had it all together. No one knew the true me. Eventually, though, this way of being broke me down.

One day, the coping methods I'd used all my life no longer worked because I was drained, exhausted, resentful, and full of shame. I needed help but I didn't trust anyone enough to let them in. I was afraid of taking up space, of being a burden; and ultimately, I was afraid of what other people would think of me. I had no idea what to do, or how to get through this. I just wanted it to end!

In therapy I was forced to look at myself – there's no escape there, as the spotlight's firmly on you – and in this space, I recognized the self-hate and shame at the heart of me, a weight I'd been carrying for years. I was disconnected from myself, from the parts of me I was ashamed of and didn't want other people to see. I was unable to live my life in the best way for me. I never felt I was good enough and would try to make myself 'enough' by pleasing others and being what I thought they wanted me to be.

I didn't have a good relationship with myself – in fact, it was terrible. I bullied myself, without even realizing what I was doing. I didn't understand that this was me living in fear of being rejected by others. But the person who was rejecting me was me!

Understanding High-Functioning Anxiety

I find it fascinating how things can change so dramatically when we start to understand ourselves. When I chose to act, it changed *everything* – my relationships, my mindset, my work life. It removed the limits I'd put on myself and unleashed a new potential. I was no longer fueled by fear of what others thought of me, or fear of failure. Of course, that fear can't be eliminated entirely, but I got better at quieting it down.

Everyone has moments of not feeling good about themselves, but when it becomes a continuous cycle that drags us down and keeps us away from happiness, it's time to act.

This is why I'm sharing my five-step guide to managing HFA with you. I want to help you learn to be comfortable about taking up space and not worry about what people might think. The goal of Step 1 of the guide is for you to gain a greater understanding of HFA, to see how its symptoms and characteristics show up, and to recognize whether they're present in your own behavior.

When I began the journey toward managing my own high-functioning anxiety, I first needed to understand what the term meant, and how this type of anxiety showed up in my life. 'High-functioning' means performing or operating at a high level; another way to describe it is 'overdelivering.' When we have HFA, we usually feel deeply unworthy, so we strive to do more just to feel as though we're 'enough' or to distract ourselves. We set the bar higher than anyone else does and get caught in a never-ending cycle in which we try to meet the standards that we've set ourselves.

The first stage in managing HFA is to understand it, and the next is to unlearn the behaviors associated with it. Why? Because I believe it's impossible to make meaningful progress without fully comprehending what it is we're working with. It's like looking at a flower and trying to understand why it's not blooming when what we really need to do is consider the whole plant.

I think most of us are aware of what anxiety is and how it can affect us. Debilitating anxiety can make us feel as though we're being held hostage by our feelings, affecting our ability to live life day-to-day or to look after ourselves properly. However, HFA is a hidden anxiety – a way of coping in shame and silence that's fueled by the fear that we're not 'good enough.'

People who suffer with HFA are often high achievers, those who, to observers, are successful, driven, and seem to have it all. This, however, is only on the outside: the part they show the world. Inside, they experience many of the symptoms of debilitating anxiety, which have become part of their being to the point where they often don't realize they're stuck in a cycle of behavior, or that they have HFA.

They learn to cope with 'not being enough' by operating to a very high standard, continually aiming to do whatever they can to show and prove their worth – not to others, but to themselves. And if they don't *understand* that they're doing this, the HFA behavior pattern continues until it culminates in exhaustion or burnout.

HFA and Heightened Sensitivity

People with HFA tend to be highly sensitive individuals. At some point(s) in their life, they've learned that who they are, or who they want to be, simply isn't good enough. They don't know how to navigate that sensitivity or realize that it leads to anxiety in the way they show up day to day, so they worry about how they're viewed, giving other people the power to define their worth. And they develop behavior patterns tied to the belief that they need to be accepted by others in order to feel they're enough.

Those with HFA 'read' the world around them using their sensitivity – taking things personally when perhaps they don't need to – and then present themselves in the way they *think* other people want them to be. They end up stuck in a cycle of 'doing' what they think others want from them, just to feel good enough, while ignoring or suppressing what they themselves truly want. They can struggle to just 'be' – to pause and be still – and this is where the problem lies. We'll look at HFA and heightened sensitivity in greater depth in Step 4.

In my work, I use a two-sided model to help my clients see the lack of understanding that those with HFA have about their sensitivity.

What Someone with HFA *Thinks* Being Sensitive Is	What Being Sensitive *Really* Is
Dramatic	Passionate
Anxious	Intuitive
Irrational	Responsive
Difficult	Empathetic
Too much	Understanding
Weak	Observant
Emotional	Attuned to others

The Two Sides of Being Sensitive

This illustrates perfectly how those of us with HFA see being sensitive as a weakness and try to dial down what we truly feel so that we fit in. We don't want to be different or to stand out, yet as humans, each of us is meant to shine in our own way, which is a beautiful thing. Sensitivity is *not* a weakness – in fact, it's where our power lies when it comes to navigating the world on a deeper, more meaningful, level.

That Isn't the Coffee I Ordered

Here's another example of how sensitivity shows up in those with HFA. I'm at the counter in a coffee shop and order a cappuccino. The barista is abrupt with me (my perception), and I feel as if I'm a burden to him because he keeps sighing as he takes my order and he hasn't smiled at me.

Then, when I receive my drink, I see it's a caffe latte instead of the cappuccino I ordered. But, because I already think I'm an annoyance and that the barista doesn't seem to be feeling his best, I don't speak up. I'm anxious about doing so because it might lead to conflict if the barista blames me for the mix-up – maybe I *did* order a latte, or I said it wrongly. So, it's easier to just deal with having the wrong drink.

What I (or my anxiety) don't consider is that the barista may not have been abrupt with me in particular. Maybe that's just how he is, or maybe he has things going on that I don't know about. But my heightened sensitivity has picked up on his manner, and my 'not good enough' belief has made it *my* fault. This is a prime example of how our beliefs color our world, and how living with HFA makes it more difficult for us to see the truth of a situation.

Rejection Sensitive Dysphoria

This emotional reaction to a perceived negative judgment is known as Rejection Sensitive Dysphoria (RSD). We see what we choose to believe about an external situation, basing this belief on our own experience rather than considering the truth of what's happening. We apply a *meaning* that may not necessarily be true, framing it in the context of our own lack of self-worth. We take something that's *external* and make it *internal,* reinforcing our feelings of not being good enough. The table below gives a few examples of how RSD shows up.

External Situation	External Situation Thought	Meaning Attributed	Internal Belief
Not being invited to a social gathering.	'They didn't invite me; I must have done something wrong.'	'They don't want to be around me.'	'I'm unlikable and unwanted.'
Not receiving a response to a message.	'They're ignoring me; I must have upset them.'	'They don't value my friendship or care about me.'	'I'm not worthy of attention or acknowledgment.'
Receiving constructive criticism at work.	'They're criticizing my work; I must be incompetent.'	'They think I'm incapable and not good enough.'	'I'm a failure and inadequate.'
Being disagreed with during a discussion.	'They disagreed with me; I must be wrong or stupid.'	'They don't respect my opinions or thoughts.'	'I'm unintelligent and inadequate.'
Not receiving a positive response from a loved one.	'They're not showing affection; I must have disappointed them.'	'They don't care about my feelings or love me.'	'I'm unlovable and unworthy of affection.'
Being interrupted during a conversation.	'They interrupted me; I must not have anything important to say.'	'They don't value my thoughts or opinions.'	'I'm unimportant and not worth listening to.'

Rejection Sensitive Dysphoria

While there's nothing wrong with me being a kind person and asking someone if they're okay, I don't have to take their troubles on board, or accept a drink I don't want simply because I'm worried about upsetting a barista. It's not my responsibility. *Reframing* how we think about an experience allows us to color the world in a different way, and to make a choice that's right for us; we'll talk more about reframing later in the book.

Our Hidden Self

When we create a persona based on fear and a need to be validated by others, it's just not sustainable. Living a life based on what we believe others are thinking about us is impossible to maintain, as we can never actually *know* what someone might think about us. Instead, all we're doing is creating a battle with ourselves – one where we're on the wrong side. We need to stop looking externally because the answers lie within. We'll look more closely at this internal battle with ourselves in Step 2.

Denying who you really are, or who you want to be, because of a learned fear about how others might see you means that you're living in a state of constant anxiety. And this can often lead to mitigating behaviors such as overthinking, catastrophizing, and perfectionism, all of which create a dysfunctional nervous system. These behaviors meet our basic need of feeling safe and secure, without addressing the underlying cause. We'll discuss these mitigating behaviors in more depth in Step 2.

Picture an iceberg. Now, it's widely understood that 90 percent of an iceberg lies below the water. So imagine, then, that the part of it that's *above* the water represents the anxiety, the fear, and the mitigating behaviors we put in place to keep ourselves safe. However, the much larger part of the iceberg, beneath the water, is the part of us that doesn't feel 'good enough.' It's the part of us that's hidden and which people cannot see.

The sad thing is that *we* are the ones who decided that part of us isn't good enough, based on our life experiences. We hide this part of ourselves away from the world, thinking we need to behave in a certain way to be accepted. This isn't the case, but nevertheless, it becomes our way of living until something hits the iceberg, forcing us to look at this hidden part of ourselves.

Not Feeling Good Enough

The one thing that every person with HFA has in common is the need to feel good enough. However, *your* version of good enough is unique to you and your learned experience, so HFA may show up differently in you than it does in someone else, making it challenging to recognize. Therefore, we need to be mindful of these differences.

The need to feel 'good enough' is the root cause of HFA, and once we understand this, we can identify the behaviors around HFA and address each one.

As I explained earlier, people with HFA tend to excel in their working life, do well socially, and are often high-performing and high-achieving individuals. However, there's a big difference between what we see and what's going on behind the scenes. On the inside, HFA sufferers experience many of the same symptoms as those with a diagnosed anxiety disorder, such as intense feelings of impending doom, the sense that things are spiraling out of control, and excessive overthinking.

They may also have physical symptoms such as a rapid heart rate or gastrointestinal problems. A familiar analogy is that of the swan gliding gracefully and calmly through life while paddling frantically beneath the surface. People who live with HFA can struggle with feelings of shame and guilt about hiding their true selves and can dislike themselves or feel unlovable. HFA can also impact their ability to form meaningful relationships.

This is what happened to me. I was living for others rather than myself, without even knowing it. I was searching for any form of connection that allowed me to feel needed – if someone wanted something from me, it meant that I was good enough. This was a formula I learned as a child from the way I related to others.

However, as an adult I brought this pattern into my relationships, never allowing myself to understand what *I* really needed, away from the validation of others. I deprived myself of the relationship depth I truly craved in order to fulfill my need of being wanted. I was only ever temporarily fulfilled with the scraps I allowed myself to receive from others, and I felt so disconnected, unseen, unheard, and lonely.

I allowed this to continue because I believed I was unworthy of love, unworthy of having my needs met. And if our needs go unmet for whatever reason, we can end up chasing this fulfillment in our relationships. We continue a pattern in which we're desperate to be seen and feel wanted and will do anything to ensure we please others, at the expense of our own time and energy. This can become exhausting.

Creating Life Rules

If while you were growing up you didn't feel loved, chances are you'll continue to seek this love in your ongoing relationships. You'll repeat the pattern until you understand *why* you're doing this and are able to develop strategies to support you moving forward. Your 'inner child' – the part of you that still holds on to those childhood experiences and colors your current existence – needs to be addressed in order to find this understanding. Only then can you begin to break free of the pattern.

> The CHILD who received conditional love = the ADULT who feels they must earn love and doesn't feel good enough.

When I went back to my own childhood to understand my patterns of behavior, I realized that my caregivers hadn't given me the emotional connection I needed. This wasn't their fault, as they'd been guided by their own early life experiences. But, because my emotional needs were not met, I learned I was 'too much' and worried about taking up space. As a result, I learned to dim my light. I learned not to trust myself and to focus more on the reactions of others to ensure I stayed 'enough' for them.

However, it wasn't that I was too much – it was that others didn't know how to hold the space for me to be me. I was a sensitive child who noticed people's reactions and interpreted them by assigning irrational meanings; this then led to me creating my own life rules and controlling the way I showed up.

As children we develop life rules about how we relate to others, based on the assumptions we make about our experiences, and these rules can continue into our adult relationships. For example, a rule you may have learned as a child was that 'people will always leave you.' You may have formed this belief because one parent was absent for some of your childhood, or repeatedly let you down. You felt as though you couldn't rely on that parent, which then subconsciously carried through to your future relationships.

> The CHILD who was left to meet their own emotional needs = the ADULT who struggles to be vulnerable with others.

HFA and Fear of Rejection

As I've explained, when we have HFA, we can feel that we're 'too sensitive.' But this isn't true. The issue lies with the fact that we don't have the right tools to navigate our sensitivity. We may be attuned to other people and notice things about them, but instead of understanding that we're picking up on something that's going on with them, we personalize it. This can then impact our own behavior.

Here's an example. You've gone into work and one of your co-workers, with whom you normally share a few laughs, is looking very serious. You crack a joke as usual, but there's no response. You immediately start to catastrophize and imagine what you might have done to hurt them, and why they no longer like you.

The truth is that you're sensitive to your co-worker's behavior, so you notice when they're not as they usually are and that something feels different; however, instead of asking them if everything's all right, you've personalized it and assumed it was something that you did. As a result, you may shut down because you feel your co-worker's rejected you (even though, in reality, that hasn't happened), or you may overcompensate in order to feel that you have them back onside.

Now, it may be that your co-worker didn't sleep well the previous night or has a difficult meeting coming up, or something going on in their personal life, and this isn't about you at all. When you *understand* your own sensitivity, so much can change. Reframing how you see such a situation is immensely powerful.

While the root cause of HFA is not feeling good enough, that feeling comes from a place of fear. This fear is based on our past experiences, something which we'll go into more fully in Step 2. As I've explained, HFA sufferers hide away the parts of themselves that they feel aren't acceptable, and their anxiety drives them on to achieve more and more. They're striving for the feeling of being *enough*, even if it's temporary, but until they can *accept* themselves as they truly are, this cannot happen. Instead, they find a way to meet their need for approval, even if doing so is detrimental to their well-being.

Your worth isn't determined by someone else's ability to appreciate it. Your worth comes from the relationship that you hold with yourself, how you respect yourself, how you listen to and offer yourself what you need, and how you protect yourself from energies that don't vibe with you.

The Importance of Self-Reflection

I'd like to make it clear that I'm not here to blame anyone for this; we're all human, each of us with our own complex needs, and sometimes the people around us don't have the ability to meet those needs. I'm grateful for all I was given during my upbringing, while at the same time understanding what I didn't receive. I was a very angry teenager, but inside I was desperate for love, desperate to be seen. Yet I didn't let anyone in.

Looking back now, I know that this behavior was rooted in fear of rejection. I learned to be alone in my head, secretly sharing my thoughts with my diary – until someone found it, after which I turned to poetry and art. I became good at putting on a mask, showing the world what I felt I needed to in order to receive validation and prove there was nothing wrong with me.

I was running from and ignoring the parts of me that I didn't accept, but I didn't realize that the battle was within me. I could have read all the self-help books in the world, each one telling me I needed to love myself, yet it was impossible for me to do that when I didn't know what was going on. I knew only one way to meet my needs, and that was to give people what I thought they wanted from me.

It worked, until it didn't. And that's when I knew things had to change. I truly believe that there are things we go through which help us grow, leading to deeper understanding. Just like the butterfly in its cocoon waiting for release, we need to spend time in this space until we're ready for change.

While we're going through life, sometimes we don't understand it until we reflect on our past and connect the dots to the present. Our experiences help us to understand our behavior patterns, offering us insightful choices to move forward. As we do so, we may continue to find ourselves in situations where we think we're drowning. But the resilience we develop through self-reflection gives us the strength and courage to continue life's path.

Knowing Who We Are

As HFA isn't a recognized mental health diagnosis, there's only limited information available on how to understand and manage it. This is something I'm changing with the five-step guide in this book. And by *change*, I don't mean simply in terms of labeling; for me, it's about *understanding*. Deep diving into your behavior will give you the insight and wisdom to help you become more conscious of yourself.

If we struggle to take up space for ourselves because we feel we're a burden, this can show up in how we relate to the world around us. It can limit and confine us in a space we feel we deserve, while not allowing ourselves to expand. You weren't born this way; you learned that this is how you need to be.

> *You can unlearn this way of living,*
> *disconnecting from how you think*
> *you* **should** *be and reconnecting*
> *into a space of* **being.**

At the age of 22, I was diagnosed with dyslexia, and it broke me. I remember sitting with a university lecturer after she'd asked to speak with me about the first essay I'd ever failed. I'd catastrophized beforehand, thinking she'd seen how stupid I really was and that I'd be thrown off my master's degree course. But what she said was, 'Lalitaa, has anyone ever spoken to you about your wording and sentences?'

When I heard those words, I lost control and cried so hard. They were tears of relief that someone had finally realized that I was struggling, yet also tears of shame at having been uncovered as a failure. There were two parts of me playing out, and this was a powerful moment. I knew that this lecturer, Sally, was speaking to me from a place of care and consideration, so on the one hand it was a pleasant feeling. But on the other, I was scrambling to hide myself.

After discovering I had dyslexia, I researched it to understand it further. However, I didn't tell anyone about my diagnosis. I realized that for years I'd found ways to cope with and manage the way I read and interpreted the world. At school and university, I'd had to work extra hard, and I constantly compared myself with other students who seemed to take things on board so easily, when I spent hours trying to get things to sink into my brain. On reflection, I could see how this impacted my self-worth and self-confidence, and why I continually masked my behaviors by striving to achieve.

That desire to achieve drove me to continue studying, so I started my doctorate. But it wasn't until after I'd completed it that I was diagnosed with attention deficit hyperactivity disorder (ADHD). Again, this broke me, but I also felt a sense of relief and remember thinking, 'It's not me' and 'I'm not the problem.' The ADHD 'label' allowed me to accept myself because it helped me to understand my mind and why I worked in the way I did.

Things finally started to make sense, and I stopped shaming myself for having something 'wrong' with me. I felt angry with my school for not picking up on the ADHD, remembering how hard I'd had to work (being the high achiever) to get top grades in my exams. At school, I'd always been the 'good' one who always followed the rules. Of course, I was praised for this behavior, which is why I continued with it.

Only when we understand who we are can we communicate with and connect to others in a grounded way, rather than by being reactive or from a highly anxious space. There's power in knowing who you are.

The Symptoms of HFA

As you now know, identifying HFA starts with recognizing and understanding its symptoms and characteristics, and knowing about the different ways it can affect us. Only with understanding can we gain acceptance. One method I use with my clients is to simply sit, without judgment and with curiosity, and help them understand themselves. Sometimes, all it takes is a mirror to help us see why we feel the way we do.

So, let's look at seven key psychological symptoms of HFA – each of which incorporates a mind/body connection – and the ways they emerge in our daily behavior. I've given an example of how each symptom can show up under the heading 'Not Feeling Good Enough,' to help you recognize it when it occurs.

HFA Symptom 1: Perfectionism

Perfectionism, or being a perfectionist, is all about how we present ourselves to the world. We hold ourselves to a high standard and have rigid expectations and specific ideas about how to achieve a desired outcome. Why? Because, deep down, we want to show everyone that we're enough.

Perfectionists tend to be driven, organized, and reliable, but they can also become overly critical when their expectations are not met. Perfectionism can also be a symptom of anxiety. Perfectionism is often rooted in fear of failure or rejection of some kind, with the fear and anxiety motivating the behavior. But the thing is, *perfect doesn't exist.*

Recently I spoke with a woman who wanted to start a business but hadn't yet done so. When I asked her why, she told me it's because she's a perfectionist. I was curious about what she meant by that, and said, 'Sometimes, when we're a perfectionist, it comes from a deeper place of fear.'

She insisted that she wasn't fearful at all, but as we continued to talk, it became clear that this wasn't the case. She explained that, despite having always been seen as strong and independent, she was afraid of failing as she didn't want to dispel other people's perception that she's 'got it together.'

Her fear that her business venture might fail came from not wanting it to appear that she wasn't 'perfect.' So, instead of taking a chance and starting her business (which she was more than capable of doing) she chose instead to stay 'safe,' stuck in the space she was in. This fear of failure, and the associated perfectionism, holds her back.

Some perfectionists can become paralyzed by fear of failure and are unable to start the task at hand. These consequences can apply to the greatest achievers of our time, who have refused to present their best work due to fear of failure and the worry that people will judge or criticize them. This is what I mean when I say that many of my clients know that something's wrong but they're not sure what it is.

This woman wanted to start a business but used her perfectionism as an excuse not to do so; however, at the root of this was fear of failure. There are many layers to this because, when we have HFA, we use our heightened sensitivity to navigate the world. Our behavior, reactions, and the way we present ourselves are based on what we've learned from past experiences, and they're designed to keep us safe. We don't even realize that we don't feel 'good enough' – we just know that something isn't quite right.

Not Feeling Good Enough

Imagine that you and I are having a conversation and, while I'm speaking, you glance away or seem distracted. As a perfectionist with HFA, I'll then change what I'm saying or how I approach the conversation because I think you're not interested in what I have to say. However, this is just my perception. You could be tired or distracted by something that's nothing to do with me.

But I need to show you that I'm 'perfect,' and that I've got everything together, as it's part of my need for control. Doing this makes me feel that I'm good enough, and that there's nothing wrong with me – even though, deep down, I know this isn't true. This is a temporary fix. Being a perfectionist means I'm not portraying myself as I truly am. Rather, I present the version I think I need to be to gain acceptance from others. And when I get that acceptance, it makes me feel better.

When we look for external validation, we give other people the power over our worthiness. It means that every move we make is done in order to satisfy someone else and how we think they want us to be, rather than doing what feels genuine to us. It's time to take back this power.

HFA Symptom 2: Catastrophizing

Catastrophizing can be described as imagining the worst possible outcome of an action or event, or believing that things are much worse than they really are. It's a form of cognitive dissonance or distorted thinking. When we catastrophize, we overanalyze a given scenario and overestimate the likelihood of something bad happening. Going down this rabbit hole can put us in a state of fear, anxiety, overwhelm, and confusion.

Feeling nervous about giving a presentation is fairly standard behavior. However, if we then imagine losing our voice, the projector not working, and the audience laughing at us, and replay these negative scenarios repeatedly in our mind, when the event happens in real life the body's already anxious, as it's experienced multiple visualizations in which things go wrong. We've created a situation where we're already connected to negative emotions, which only makes our anxiety worse. This is because our imagination has been let loose down the rabbit hole.

Catastrophizing comes from fear of judgment, which stems from fear of rejection. It limits us and prevents us from achieving our full potential.

We learn to catastrophize – to think 10 steps ahead – because it keeps us safe. If we can identify all the things that might go wrong, in all the possible scenarios, it means we can plan for them and avoid them. But this can stop us from taking opportunities, as we've already imagined our way out of them. We're letting our fear guide our path forward. If we overprepare ourselves for everything, it means we feel in control and don't get caught out.

We do this to avoid feeling emotions such as distress, shame, guilt, or embarrassment again. I say 'again,' because in the past we *have* felt these emotions and it wasn't nice, so now we find ways to avoid them. It's the same sort of thing that we learn, for example, after touching a sharp knife and cutting a finger. We don't want to get hurt again, so we become more careful when we use sharp knives. Our brain associates the knife with pain, so it perceives it as a danger. Or perhaps someone laughed at us at school when we spoke up in class about something and we felt embarrassed and ashamed, so we avoid speaking up again to avoid a repeat of those feelings.

But when we catastrophize and overthink a situation, we start creating boundaries and emotions that don't actually exist. And as our body doesn't know the difference between what's real and what's imaginary, as we catastrophize, it thinks we're really experiencing these *imaginary* emotions.

For example, if we think things like *If I don't pass this test, I'll fail the class. Then I won't get into college, and I'll never have a career;* or *If my work isn't flawless, I'll never be promoted, and then I'll be a failure at my job;* or even *If I don't make a good impression, everyone will laugh at me and I'll be an outcast,* our body thinks that this is what's happening and tries to keep us safe by teaching us to avoid the situation.

Not Feeling Good Enough

Imagine you've just bought a colorful top and are intending to wear it on a night out. But then you remember a time when someone else wore something similar, and a friend commented on it in a negative way. You imagine her saying to you, 'Oh, are you wearing that? It's a bit bright, isn't it?'

These things you're thinking about haven't happened, and yet you've still experienced the emotions of embarrassment and hurt. You're already catastrophizing, imagining judgment where there is none and overthinking the situation. Then, when you're getting ready to go out, you become anxious because you don't want to experience those negative feelings again. So, you decide not to wear the new top.

This kind of 10-steps-ahead thinking creates a lot of anxiety and fear, and it means you're not living in the way you need to live. You care so much about what other people think because you want them to see you as enough. However, you can learn to navigate this overthinking so it no longer holds you back – I'll show you how to do this in Step 3, when we put together a HFA tool kit, and in Step 4, when we look at setting healthy boundaries.

HFA Symptom 3: Fear of Judgment

Fear of judgment comes from a place where we worry far too much about what other people think. We don't want anyone to see us in a 'bad' way and so we allow other people to define our worth, even though, as I've explained, this isn't where our true worth lies. We become tied to others, making choices based on what we think *they* want to see.

> *There will always be things we'll fail at and people who don't like us. We need to be okay with that because the alternative is living a life where we constantly chase external validation.*

Fear of judgment relates to our need to survive in society. For our prehistoric ancestors, being evaluated favorably rather than judged for any shortcomings would have meant a higher chance of survival. Think about it: even today, success at work propagates a career, whereas poor performance may put you at risk of redundancy or demotion.

We can't carry the expectation that everyone will like us and say nice things about us, or that we'll succeed at everything we try; nor can we twist ourselves in knots trying to become that person. This isn't how life works, and we're worth so much more. We learn far more from failing – from falling down and getting up again – than we do from holding back parts of ourselves and not taking chances so that doesn't happen. Failing is how we learn about our resilience and what we're truly capable of. We need to be okay with flowing with what comes rather than trying hard to hold on to something over which we have no control.

Not Feeling Good Enough

Imagine that you're a part of an orchard in which every tree is an apple tree producing beautiful blossom followed by plenty of lovely fruit. But you are different. Your flowers are different, your fruit is different, and you look and smell different, and that's because you're an orange tree.

You're so worried about what the other trees will think of you that you hide away your orange-tree nature, producing apples like the other trees just to fit in. But it feels as if you're fighting a losing battle because you're an orange tree. You know you're not in sync.

This fear of failing drives you to push yourself further, to produce the very best apples in the orchard (high-functioning), all the while hiding away your beautiful orange-tree self – simply because you don't wish to be judged for who you really are. But you're an orange tree not an apple tree, and you can't keep this up forever. This isn't a natural state of being, and it will harm you in the long run.

HFA Symptom 4: Anticipatory Anxiety

The term 'anticipatory anxiety' is another way of describing a feeling of fear and worry around bad things that *could* happen. It can be experienced in many different contexts, but it commonly focuses on things you can't predict or control. With anticipatory anxiety, you might spend a lot of time imagining worst-case scenarios. Overfocusing on these unwanted outcomes can increase your frustration and sense of hopelessness.

Certainly, we've all experienced anticipatory anxiety at one time or another – before a job interview, a first date, a school exam, or a major trip – but if it becomes part of our everyday interactions, it can be debilitating. Anticipatory anxiety is worry and fear about the future – the fear that bad things might happen, or that you might become unable to successfully accomplish what you set out to do. It's the anxiety we feel when we're anticipating a difficult decision, action, or situation.

Anticipatory anxiety can make you feel exhausted as you search for ways to avoid the experiences you fear. It's far more than simply butterflies in the stomach or a touch of apprehension. People who live with HFA may experience extreme anxiety prior to events, sending them into a fear-based state of high adrenaline without the ability to think clearly.

It's difficult to function in such a state and, just as we saw in the section about catastrophizing and worrying about what might potentially happen, this leads to behavior where we imagine various different scenarios, thinking 10 steps ahead. But the body doesn't want to feel anxiety; it wants to protect us from that. So, it stops us from doing things we might otherwise have done, simply because of what *might* happen.

Not Feeling Good Enough

Imagine your partner's been a little preoccupied lately, but when you mention it, they insist there's nothing's wrong. However, you don't believe them and start to worry that they want to end the relationship. Before long, you can't stop imagining the break-up conversation that you believe is forthcoming. Thinking about losing your partner makes you feel sick, and you have trouble eating and sleeping normally. However, understanding that this is your heightened sensitivity coming into play allows you to stop this pattern before it begins.

HFA Symptom 5: Being Over-Responsible

Responsible people care about others and are seen as committed, dependable, and accountable. But it's easy to go too far and become *over*-responsible. Being over-responsible means you people-please and suppress your own needs in order to prioritize those of others and to minimize or eliminate conflict, criticism, rejection, disappointment, and loss.

Being over-responsible also means that you find it difficult to trust others and prefer to take responsibility for things yourself. Over-responsible people are those who take on excessive responsibility and burdens, often for others. They also don't want to let anyone down because of fear of rejection, and they may feel compelled to fix problems, even if they aren't responsible for them. So, they keep showing up, keep saying 'yes, I can do this,' because as long as they can manage all these different things, they'll be 'okay.'

When we have HFA, being over-responsible is rooted in the need to please or care for others. This desire often stems from a deep need for love and approval. We become trapped in a pattern where we don't want to say 'no' to anyone because doing so means we're letting people down, even if they're not our responsibility.

It also means that people will like us and appreciate what we do, feeding our need for external approval. If we can take on everything and make sure it's done correctly, we feel as though we're seen as good enough because of all we achieve. We then learn that, to get this feeling again, we need to overachieve. This becomes a repetitive pattern of behavior that feeds our need for validation.

Not Feeling Good Enough

Imagine you're at work and your manager asks you to take on a task. You accept it, but then in a team meeting he asks you to do something else as well. You already have a full schedule that day and you've also arranged to go out with your friends after work, but you're reluctant to say 'no' as you don't want to let your manager down or have the team judge you negatively.

However, at the same time, you don't want to cancel on your friends because you want to avoid them thinking you don't care about them. So, you turn up to meet them feeling overwhelmed, exhausted, and overstretched, and then go home and try to do some work, waking up early the next morning to try and finish it. No one sees the hours you're putting in, and you feel so tired and stuck on this hamster wheel.

This is the point where over-responsibility breaks down, as it's not sustainable in the long term. We need to learn the limits of what we can manage and enforce those limits.

HFA Symptom 6: Overachieving

Setting goals and reaching them is, for most people, a part of life, and it can be very satisfying to work toward a reward or an achievement. However, for a person with HFA, achieving things is simply part of the process they've set up to feed their need for external validation. They're not able to take the time to appreciate what they've done, nor can they stop taking on more and more challenges. This is because the void inside them can never be satisfied by simply achieving.

The positive feelings they experience from reaching their goal are fleeting because they rely on the praise that they receive from others to feel good enough rather than their personal pride or sense of achievement. Thus, the pattern continues, based on this flawed perception.

If we keep achieving, it means that other people will like us and appreciate what we do, which feeds our need for approval. If we can control everything and make sure it's done correctly, we feel as though we're seen as 'good enough' because of all we achieve. We then learn that, in order to get this feeling, we need to *over*achieve.

Not Feeling Good Enough

One of my clients, 'Lucy,' is a senior consultant at her firm; she's one of the youngest to reach this level and is seen as a role model. However, inside she's filled with self-doubt and worry, often spending hours organizing and preparing for meetings. Although she comes across as calm, organized, and confident, no one sees all the extra effort she puts in behind closed doors.

Deep down, Lucy feels that there's nothing to her. She believes she's not as good as the other consultants and spends a lot of time reading up about leadership. She takes on more work than she can handle because she doesn't feel good enough and wants to show others that she's capable and deserving of her role. She also attends every work-related social event, even if she doesn't really have the time, because she wants to fit in. People see her as bubbly and talkative, but what they don't notice is that she struggles to have conversations and is using alcohol to give her the energy and confidence to get through the event.

Lucy is a high-achieving individual, but she's fueled from a place of not feeling good enough. This leads to overachieving behavior as she takes on more to show her worth to others, regardless of how she truly feels. Her battle is with herself.

HFA Symptom 7: A Need for Control

For some people, the need to control everything in their life can become all-consuming and exhausting. A person with HFA may have trouble coping when things don't go to plan or when there are unexpected changes. They also tend to be highly organized, structured, and self-disciplined, finding comfort in predictability and structure.

Needing to feel in control comes from a lack of self-trust. We may have a need to control everything around us in order to feel at peace, and we may not trust anyone else to handle things in a different way. Letting go of control is hard. In times of uncertainty, people feel safer when they have a sense of control and this often leads to attempts to control outcomes, situations, others' reactions, or even the environment. The more uncertain the situation, the more people cling to their attempts to control it.

Usually, we get into this pattern because we're trying to avoid a difficult feeling. Anxiety, for example, can be caused by feeling a lack of control in one or more areas of life. When this happens, we focus extra hard on the things we *can* control, putting behaviors in place to help us manage this focus.

This is how we cope in a world where we might not be getting the support we need. These behaviors can give us a sense of relief or a way to avoid difficult feelings, but this relief is only temporary because sooner or later those difficult feelings come back, and we feel like we need to do that thing again. This pattern can be hard to break free from but with the right support you can do it.

Not Feeling Good Enough

Imagine you're driving a train along a track. There are other people on the train with you, all of whom can help with the driving, but you need to be the one who drives, all the time. You ignore all offers to help by giving you a break or doing any associated driving tasks. Instead, you keep pressing on, even though you're getting tired and, in fact, you wouldn't mind some help.

However, giving up the wheel means giving up control over your situation and where you're going. What if the other people drive too fast and the train derails? Or they decide to take a different track to a different destination without telling you? It just doesn't feel safe. So, instead of trusting those around you, you keep on driving, even though you're lonely and exhausted, until the train breaks down. It's better that way, staying in control.

So, there you have it – the HFA Seven. Did any of these symptoms resonate with you? Can you recognize your own behavior within the examples here? Perhaps they all spoke to you. After all, each of the seven are connected – they all link back to wanting to feel safe, something that perhaps we didn't experience when we were young. While it's normal to have times when we feel like this, it's not normal for it to be a state of being. That's when it becomes debilitating and exhausting.

The Two-Sided Behavior of HFA

This all sounds reasonable, you might be thinking, but how do I apply it to me? Okay, let's dig deeper. Essentially, people with HFA can be said to have two sides to them: the 'learned side,' which is the part they present to the world, and the 'shadow side,' which is the part they keep hidden away. The 'learned side' (the high-functioning side) gets them the validation they need to feel safe and in control, but it's in the 'shadow side' where all their fears, worries, and anxiety live. The way I see it, our shadow's always with us, but we don't see it until the sun shines. This table shows some of the ways these two sides of us can manifest:

Learned Side (What We Show)	Shadow Side (What We Hide)
Organized	Excessive worrier
Sociable	Perfectionist
Hardworking	Often exhausted
Meets all deadlines	Fears failure
High achiever	Concerned about disappointing others
Proactive	Procrastinator
Appears calm	Has trouble sleeping
Overachiever	Inadequate
Successful	Fearful
Appears to have got it together	Difficulty setting boundaries/ saying 'no'
Helpful	Burned-out
Empathetic	Over-responsible
Problem solver	Lonely

The Learned Side vs. the Shadow Side

When I started my journey toward understanding my experience of HFA, all I knew was that I didn't want to face my shadow side. I was embarrassed about feeling anxious, so I only showed the world what I thought it would love, appreciate, and value. Of course, we all do this to some extent, but there comes a point when the pressure to appear perfect, and to avoid failure, judgment, or disappointing others, takes over to such an extent that we break down.

It's not possible to lock away our true selves indefinitely. Continually ignoring our own desires and boundaries can only lead to exhaustion and anxiety, and a constant feeling that something's wrong. Behavior that may have started out as positive – such as taking responsibility, being a high achiever, or always being the 'calm one' – will catch up with us eventually. However, there's a better way of living – one where we're grounded and able to 'just be,' without fear driving us through life.

In this section, we'll explore seven of the most common types of two-sided behavior linked to HFA, seeing how their symptoms manifest and how we can learn to recognize them when they do. I've also given my analysis of each HFA behavior type and explained how it can affect us. As an example, I've included a real-life client case study; so, let me introduce you to 'Sara.'

CASE STUDY

Sara was an executive at a law firm and someone who performed well. Yet when she came to see me, she spoke of experiencing extreme levels of anxiety that were impairing her quality of life. She suffered from overthinking, which led to self-doubt, and her need to overachieve often left her feeling exhausted.

Sara presented as a driver in her workplace, often taking the lead on projects, but in the background, she struggled to maintain a work-life balance. At home she'd catch up with work and didn't have time to do the things she wanted to do. She rarely took her annual leave, and when she did, it was only if she'd pre-booked a trip.

While she appeared successful and accomplished from the outside, Sara's anxiety was interfering with both her professional and personal life. She struggled with setting boundaries, managing feelings of guilt, and maintaining a romantic relationship. She also told me that she felt worn down by her brain thinking about multiple work-related scenarios.

As you read about the types of two-sided behavior (below) and ask yourself the 'questions for self-reflection' at the end of each one, take a moment to consider if they apply to you and your own patterns of behavior. Be honest, and you might be surprised at what you discover about yourself.

HFA Behavior Type 1

The over-responsible one vs. the one who can manage everything

To the outside world, being responsible for yourself, your life, and other people (or even budgets, systems, and teams) means that you've got it together. You seem calm, in control, and able to manage multiple things. Being responsible is a show of empathy, proof that you care about people, situations, and things.

However, for those who struggle with HFA it's easy to go too far and take on everyone else's tasks, their mistakes, and even their emotions. Attuning our own needs to those of others is how we've kept ourselves safe in the past – to the point where we might no longer realize we're doing it. But when we consistently do this, we may start to find it challenging to distinguish between our own feelings and those of the people around us, and this can lead to emotional exhaustion and a blurred sense of self. This is *over-responsibility*.

When we become over-responsible, we feel guilty when things go wrong, even if they're outside our control. And while we gain deep satisfaction from handling it all and fixing whatever comes our way, when we take on too much, it can lead to exhaustion, stress, and burnout. A person who's over-responsible may feel overburdened and struggle to switch off.

CASE STUDY

Sara talked about having so much work to do, but when we broke it down, we found that much of it was things she had to do for other people. If someone asked her to take on a task for them, she felt guilty saying 'no,' as she struggled with setting boundaries. So, she'd often overload her desk and diary with other people's work.

On one occasion, when a colleague was on sick leave and his manager was worried about redistributing the work, Sara took on all of the additional tasks herself. This meant she was doing two jobs and, as a result, was exhausted. When we discussed this, she disclosed that she felt bad for the manager and wanted to make her feel good. However, she did so at the expense of her own well-being.

Analysis

Taking on everyone else's responsibilities is often a sign of conflict avoidance. In trying to keep the peace, we'd rather shoulder more than our fair share of the burden than risk a difficult conversation or a confrontation that might involve anger or rejection. This often stems from our childhood environment and is carried into adulthood and adult relationships, be they romantic, work, or friendships.

Behavior Pattern

Being over-responsible can be a hard habit to break, as it gets reinforced externally by those who depend on you, and internally by your need to feel competent and avoid conflict. Yet the more responsibility you take on, the more exhausted you feel as you try to keep all the plates spinning, feeling guilty if one of them falls. This is neither sustainable nor good for you.

Questions for Self-Reflection

- *Do you tend to take on everyone else's tasks?*

- *If someone you love is grumpy, do you assume it's because of something you've done?*

- *Do you take on other people's mistakes or emotions?*

HFA Behavior Type 2

The controller vs. the high achiever

As we discussed earlier, people who live with HFA are often overachievers. They tend to have high-powered or influential jobs or high levels of responsibility within their organization. They're usually well-regarded by their colleagues, managers, and employees because they do a great job and always seem to succeed at whatever they turn their hand to. However, on the inside they're trying to control one, multiple, or all aspects of their lives.

While being in control of your life can be a positive thing, for some people, the desire to control everything can become all-consuming and exhausting. It's also important to recognize that this need for control can manifest differently for everyone. One person with HFA may have trouble coping when things don't go to plan, while another may struggle to show their true emotions to others.

CASE STUDY

Sara said she was exhausted by her brain going over all the possible situations that could play out at work. Once, her manager asked her to arrange a meeting without telling her what it was for. Sara instantly felt anxious and started visualizing her manager sacking her.

She told me that if she'd known what the meeting was about, it would have helped her to feel more in control, as she could have planned for it. Instead, the not-knowing led to a sinking feeling and increasing anxiety as she wondered whether she'd be able to manage the meeting successfully. She felt out of control, and worrying about what other people might think added to her fear.

Analysis

The desire for control may be rooted in fear of uncertainty; it can also come from an overwhelming sense that life's spinning out of control. One way to deal with this feeling is to seek control in other areas. While uncertainty is part of life, for some people it can be difficult to manage and leads to an intense need to control everything around them.

Uncertainty can also mean more space for worrying and overthinking. As a result, those with HFA may try to self-soothe by controlling as many outcomes as they can to alleviate their worries. Feeling unable to control the world and their circumstances, they instead seek to control themselves and anything within their grasp.

Behavior Pattern

The need for control can come from not trusting other people to complete tasks. This means we often take on the responsibility ourselves and end up doing it all. And of course, because we do such a good job, it adds to the perception of us as a 'high achiever.' The more we control, the more we achieve, and it becomes an endless and often exhausting cycle of achieving more because we're controlling more.

Questions for Self-Reflection

- *Do you feel that you give your all to everything you do?*

- *Do you trust others to complete tasks?*

- *Do you feel that you're better off doing things by yourself?*

HFA Behavior Type 3

The perfectionist vs. the hard worker

There's a perception that being a perfectionist means you care deeply about things and people, that you're in control and you can take responsibility. To the outside viewer, a perfectionist seems diligent and methodical, someone who rarely makes mistakes and who pays close attention to detail. A perfectionist can be trusted to do things well, as they're seen as hard workers with high standards.

When this desire for perfection is healthy, it can be very motivating and drive people to achieve success. However, when perfectionism becomes unhealthy, it's a fast track to lasting anxiety. The HFA perfectionist sets unrealistically high standards for themselves and others, which leads to feelings of anxiety, dissatisfaction, and resentment if these standards aren't met. It also means they're quick to find fault with themselves and are overly critical of their mistakes. It can be difficult for them to accept compliments from others or celebrate successes.

CASE STUDY

When Sara first came to therapy, I asked her what she wanted from the sessions. 'I want to be fixed,' she said. 'Why do you feel that you're broken?' I asked. 'Because I'm not a success and I'm not achieving my goals,' she replied.

However, Sara was perceived as a high achiever by her peers and had won awards for her work. When we explored her response further, it became clear that she had very high expectations of herself and, when she didn't reach these standards, she'd mentally castigate herself. Sara found it very difficult to have self-compassion, so it was natural for her inner critic to emerge in many situations and criticize her for not being 'perfect.'

Analysis

Lurking beneath a perfectionist's finely tuned exterior is usually a people-pleaser. While perfectionism is often the result of trying to live up to an internal ideal, it can also be motivated by fear of how others perceive you. Another root cause is a deep-seated fear of failure, which leads to an almost obsessive need to control every aspect of your life. Constantly striving for perfection is another defense mechanism for dealing with uncertainty.

Behavior Pattern

The impossible task of trying to please everyone else *and* meet their own impossibly high standards leaves the HFA perfectionist physically and emotionally exhausted. It can take a toll on their relationships and even lead to burnout. Perfectionists either procrastinate over tasks to avoid failure or struggle to take breaks because they're so focused on doing a thorough job and getting it right. As a result, it always feels as though there's more to be done or perfected, which sends them back on their endless journey.

Questions for Self-Reflection

- *Do you find it difficult to receive criticism from others?*

- *Is it hard for you to take a break from work?*

- *Do you have high standards for yourself and others?*

HFA Behavior Type 4

The excessive worrier vs. the unflappable one

A certain amount of worry, doubt, and anxiety is a normal part of life. It's natural to worry about an unpaid bill, an upcoming job interview, or meeting someone for the first time. In fact, doing so shows that we're human and not coldhearted robots. People with HFA appear confident and not overly stressed on the surface, so when we exhibit a small amount of worry it simply reads as being caring, compassionate, and diligent – all while remaining calm and unflappable.

However, while we might appear this way on the outside, we are in fact overanalyzing everything in our head. We carry constant background worry about every single conversation, decision, and action. This nonstop worrying leads to stress, panic, and anxiety, but no one ever realizes this because we appear so calm. This makes us feel isolated and as though our true selves wouldn't be accepted, leading to feelings of shame and the need to hide ourselves.

CASE STUDY

During one of our sessions, Sara said, 'I feel like my brain's always on, but other people can't see it.' Yet she didn't want anyone to know her thoughts because she was embarrassed by them, feeling that something was wrong with her. When I asked her what she thought was wrong, she replied, 'No one will like me. I'm so boring and people won't think I'm fun.'

This underlying belief was being carried with her, causing her to scan situations out of fear of rejection. In one instance, she was meeting a friend for coffee and the friend was running late. However, instead of simply waiting calmly for her friend to arrive, Sara spent the time worrying excessively that she wasn't going to show up and wondering what the other customers thought of her being in the coffee shop alone.

Analysis

Excessive worrying can be described as the feeling that something, someone, or a situation is far worse than the reality turns out to be. Fear is the root cause of this worry; and this is because our brain is constantly asking 'what if?' questions: 'What if I fail? What if this doesn't work? What if this is wrong? What if they don't like it? What if they get mad at me?' And because the brain interprets uncertainty as danger, something as simple as making a typo in a work email quickly escalates into us being 'fired.'

Behavior Pattern

With each 'what if?' question, the brain goes down a rabbit hole of scenarios and possibilities, and before you know it, your anxiety has completely taken over. This can be exhausting, especially when it becomes difficult to manage these thoughts. Even worse, it then turns into an automatic process within the brain because we become so used to doing it that we default to this behavior, which perpetuates the pattern.

Questions for Self-Reflection

- *Have you noticed that you overthink situations?*

- *Do you have 'what if?' thoughts that overwhelm you?*

- *Do others see you as the calm one?*

HFA Behavior Type 5
The fearful one vs. the successful one

Many of us are afraid of failing, at least some of the time. In a healthy form, fear of failure can spur us to work hard and try hard, which in turns means that we achieve more and become successful. This is why people with HFA often become high achievers and are perceived as very successful people who are widely respected.

However, in an unhealthy form, fear of failure stops us from doing the things that will move us forward. Because we're so afraid that we'll try and not succeed, we decide not to try at all. This way, we prevent any potential pain, embarrassment, or disappointment. However, we also prevent ourselves from chasing our dreams and we limit our own potential.

CASE STUDY

Sara told me that she kept a mental file filled with all her perceived failures – the things for which she'd never forgiven herself. When she first started therapy, she'd also blame herself for things that didn't work out. In one instance, she went on a date and thought it had gone well, but a few days later she was ghosted. 'I replayed over and over again what I could have done wrong,' she said. She also kept thinking of the things she could have done differently to avoid her perceived failure and felt upset and angry with herself.

Analysis

Fear of failure may develop for many reasons, from growing up with a critical parent or a dysfunctional family to experiencing bullying or a traumatic event. If you've ever failed at something and, as a result, felt humiliated or upset, these emotions may have stayed with you long after the event itself. However, it's important to understand that these feelings relate more to your *perception* of failure and what it means to you than to the failure itself. Because of this, failure often manifests as a feeling long before it becomes an actual experience.

Behavior Pattern

When we fail, it's accompanied by a variety of emotions, none of them pleasant. Embarrassment, anxiety, anger, sadness, and shame are all part of the experience and, therefore, we'll often do anything we can to avoid feeling this way. We end up chasing success relentlessly until we become exhausted, or we may avoid chasing any kind of success at all. In the former scenario, achieving success may make us even more scared to fail. In the latter, it may make us even more scared to try.

Questions for Self-Reflection

- *Do you worry about failing?*

- *Do you worry about what others think of you?*

- *Do you struggle to feel proud of your achievements?*

HFA Behavior Type 6

The disappointer vs. the one with healthy boundaries

It's a good thing to be caring and accommodating when people ask for your support, especially loved ones. Saying yes when asked for help, or going the extra mile just so other people aren't let down, even when it takes a lot of effort, makes you seem considerate. As we've previously established, external validation is very important to HFA sufferers, as it's part of what helps us to feel good enough. However, once again, it's important to recognize that this feeling is external and that we sometimes seek it at the expense of what we truly want.

Not wanting to disappoint others can lead to people-pleasing behavior – an inability to say no and a lack of boundaries. This in turn can result in us feeling stressed, burned-out, and overworked, as we prioritize the needs of others over meeting our own. It can also lead to feelings of resentment toward others and a continual erosion of boundaries.

CASE STUDY

Sara had poor boundaries, which led to feelings of anxiety. At the time of our sessions, she was living with her sister, who would often come into her room and start talking, even when Sara had work to do. When I asked Sara why she didn't tell her sister she was busy, she replied, 'I don't want to let her down or disappoint her.'

As a result, Sara overextended herself and often had to stay awake until late at night to finish her work. She took responsibility for her sister's feelings, allowing her to blur boundaries simply to keep her happy. When we explored this together, Sara realized that she let lots of people treat her this way and always wanted to appear 'available' for fear of disappointing others.

Analysis

Disappointment is a complex emotion that can be hard to process. It encompasses a range of uncomfortable feelings, such as loss, grief, shame, embarrassment, anger, frustration, and fear. When we worry about disappointing others, we're actually worrying about people not accepting us and ultimately rejecting who we truly are.

Therefore, to gain others' acceptance, we try constantly to please them and struggle to say 'no,' which can lead to a blurring of our boundaries. Boundaries define who we are and who we're not, dictating who and what we allow into our lives and what we keep out. Letting others trample on those boundaries simply because we don't want to disappoint them is, essentially, denying our true self. (We'll talk a lot more about boundaries in Step 4.)

Behavior Pattern

When we allow the fear of disappointing others to take over our own behavior, it's like banging our head against a wall because, despite our best efforts, we can't control what people think of us. One of the things about disappointment is that it's very personal. People have a variety of reasons for reacting the way they do to a situation, and something that feels like a big deal to you may not be that way for someone else, which makes it even more difficult to process. We end up stuck in an ultimately futile pattern of trying to please others when in fact we can't control the outcome or their response to it.

Questions for Self-Reflection

- *Do you worry about upsetting others?*

- *Do you struggle to say no to others?*

- *Are you concerned about letting others down?*

HFA Behavior Type 7
The overachiever vs. the one who has it all

When we constantly push ourselves to achieve our goals, we can be seen by others as inspirational, or as someone who 'has it all.' Don't get me wrong; working hard to achieve your ambitions is a wonderful and enriching part of life's journey, as well as a great opportunity to learn, but the issue lies in whether the goals you chase are things you desire with your whole heart or whether they feed a need for validation and praise from others, to show that you're good enough.

With HFA, this need for external approval means that nothing you achieve will ever be enough because the positive feelings you're chasing come from the outside rather than from within; from the praise of others rather than the satisfaction of achieving a goal you deeply desire. It can lead to a pattern of constantly taking on more and more, until you burn out completely. It's not sustainable.

CASE STUDY

Sara had been named employee of the year, as well as achieving other awards and accolades in the workplace. Yet she constantly strove to become 'better' at what she did; to be seen as the person who got things done, no matter how many extra hours it took.

While this led to a great deal of praise and validation in the office, her personal life suffered as a result. She worked so hard that she had no time for herself or relationships with others, whether friend, family, or romantic. Her anxiety was overwhelming, yet she couldn't stop taking on extra work.

Analysis

There's nothing wrong with working hard to manifest your dreams. However, when this work takes over your life to the point where there's no space for anything else, or to consider whether it's what you really want to do, then it becomes a problem. It's like the snake chasing its tail; a cycle that goes round again and again, a continual pursuit of approval and achievement with no lasting payout. Sara was so concerned with making sure that others thought she was good enough that she forgot to take time for herself and was pushing toward burnout.

Behavior Pattern

Chasing validation from others can be compared to chasing a high from a drug. Its effects, while pleasurable in the moment, are fleeting, and cause us to take on more and more in order to feel the same way again. Sara liked being told she was good enough, because it fed her need for approval from others, and so she pushed herself harder and harder to become the best at what she did, to the detriment of her personal life and mental health.

Questions for Self-Reflection

- *Do you always push yourself to go that extra mile, even when you don't have the energy to do so?*

- *Do you take on tasks even when you don't want to?*

- *Do you ever feel exhausted and/or burned-out?*

Taking Stock

Take a moment to reflect. Do any of these two-sided behaviors resonate with you and your own experience? Can you detect patterns that you may not have noticed before? I remember the first time I began to understand my own patterns. It was a lightbulb moment for me. While it didn't make managing my emotions any easier at the time, or give me an excuse for my behavior, what it did do was give me answers. I was able to stop blaming myself and wondering what was wrong with me. It was the beginning of change in my life.

STEP 1 SUMMARY

Let's recap on what we've covered in Step 1. You've learned what HFA is, and how it can manifest differently from person to person, as well as some of its causes. We've looked at the seven main psychological symptoms of HFA and discussed its two-sided behavioral aspects. Step 1 is designed to open your eyes to how HFA can show up and to consider whether you can relate to it. Remember, it's perfectly okay to experience these feelings sometimes. What isn't okay is when they take over and affect our quality of life.

Recognizing that you have HFA is just the beginning. Next, you need to connect the version of you that you present to the world with the beautiful version of you waiting to be discovered inside; this is where you'll find a greater understanding of who you are and all the answers you need. It's going to take work. However, if you've read to this point, you're already on your way. Well done for sticking with the process. Let's dive into Step 2.

STEP 2

Decode Your Patterns, Uncover Your Beliefs, and Face Your Shadow

Now that you know more about HFA and its associated symptoms and behavior patterns, and have reflected on how these show up in your own life, it's time to dig deeper. In this step, we'll explore the subconscious to gain greater knowledge of our patterns and *why* we live in the way we do. We'll also look at how our past experiences can influence how we feel in the present, and why we might feel as though we're not good enough.

Just as an archaeologist descends through layers of the past, we'll explore the layers of your existence to uncover the origins of your HFA. This will then give you the insight you need to move forward along your aligned path.

Going Back to the Past to Move Forward

This book is about releasing old modes of thinking and habitual thought patterns and replacing them with fresh attitudes and insights, and the ability to look at life from a different perspective. By going back into our past to discover how HFA can develop, we'll rediscover an aspect of our nature that's not yet integrated into our conscious awareness – because we've been ignoring it or have perhaps been unaware it's even there. It's as though we're a jigsaw but we only have the pieces, not the box with the picture on it. Only when we gain understanding will we be able to see that picture.

Until then, we may feel incomplete or as though something's missing. That feeling might have driven us into an intense and restless search for anything to fill the gap, even if it meant losing ourselves along the way. We've chased the temporary fix of feeling 'enough' by doing what we think others want of us – not being able to say 'no' – or worrying about what others think. This behavior is what stops us from taking up space and following the path we want for ourselves, not for anyone else.

We keep busy so we never have to be with our thoughts, using things like drugs, sex, alcohol, overworking, or even just looking at our phone to escape. Because we struggle to be in our own mind, we find ways in the physical world to keep ourselves disconnected. We ignore the parts of ourselves that we don't accept because we don't know any other way of managing them or even realize we're struggling.

Perhaps we stay in a relationship just so we don't feel lonely or socialize with friends with whom we don't have meaningful connections because having something to do, whether it fulfills us or not, is better than nothing. Or perhaps we develop emotional eating as a way to regulate our feelings. We make sure we don't have time to reflect on ourselves, even though we know we don't fit or aren't connecting in the way we'd like to. Instead, we continue to maintain this way of living, so we don't have time to feel the pain or emptiness we carry, deep within our hearts.

You Can't Run from Yourself

You can think of this as like taking painkillers. While they might numb the pain, they don't address what's causing the pain. And if we ignore that root cause and keep taking more painkillers, after a while we become tolerant to them and need to take even more to achieve the same effect. When we have HFA, we keep using things to distract ourselves rather than going inward. However, these distractions are like the painkillers – they don't address the root cause of our HFA.

But none of this is sustainable. Regardless of what you do, these feelings will remain. If you've lived your life focusing on your achievements in the outer world and seeking external validation, it usually means that the inner world of feelings – where you find the need for real intimacy, closeness, and relationship fulfillment – has been relegated to second place. The aspects of your existence that are supposed to provide your greatest sense of security instead make you feel threatened, and you project your inner apprehension about moving forward onto your environment.

But you can't keep running from yourself. If, while you were growing up, you learned that doing certain things or behaving in a particular way meant you were praised, then you'll have continued those behaviors. Being praised makes us feel good, and we associate it with being seen and validated – and ultimately, loved.

As an adult, we make these patterns part of our way of life because we've learned that being a high achiever means we'll be praised, and people will be happy. We think that people being happy means we're enough. The other side of this is that, if we upset someone, we see it as rejection and, ultimately, as us not being enough.

When I was a child, my parents sent me for extra tuition outside school. My education was important to them, as this was something they hadn't had the chance to pursue themselves. They wanted the best for me and so I pushed myself to be the best I could be at school. I wanted to make them happy because if I wasn't doing well, they wouldn't have been okay with that and would have tried other ways to help me.

I became a high achiever, and I also knew this meant the teachers would praise me. That became my way of being, and I'd make sure I followed all the rules of doing the best I could, based on what my teachers and parents wanted from me. When I think back now, I can see how easy it is to get caught in a pattern like this.

These patterns of behavior, formed from our past experiences, keep driving us forward. It certainly drove me onto the next thing and then the next, without ever stopping to figure out what *I* wanted. I never realized that this was something I could do.

Integrating the Two Sides of You

The only way to truly escape this way of being involves going deeper, facing the pain and the darkness. Of course, this is scary, and often we avoid it because it feels bigger than it is, and it means letting go of everything we use to feel in control. Releasing these old patterns of behavior can feel a bit like being told the sky is green, not blue.

Another thing to remember is that, sometimes, we don't know that we're stuck in these behavior patterns. It's only when something happens where the old rules don't work anymore that we realize something's wrong and are forced to seek something different. This is when we can go inward to the root cause rather than just feeding the symptoms.

> *Change can be frightening. But not as frightening as staying in a place where you aren't happy and are living in fear.*

In this step, I'll help you to rediscover those parts of you with which you haven't been in touch – the aspects of your nature you've denied or kept hidden due to fear and shame. I'm not saying you did this consciously; rather, it's more likely you've never realized this has been happening. Hiding these feelings away has become a coping strategy, to the point where it's completely unintentional.

But now it's time to pull back the curtain and look at *all* your emotions and qualities, including those you don't like very much, such as jealousy, envy, greed, or the part of you that's fearful, dependent, or competitive. This is our 'shadow side,' which we touched on in Step 1. We're connected to this part of us, yet it remains hidden. It's easy to feel ashamed of your shadow side, as it's the part of you that you're afraid will be rejected if it's ever exposed.

In the past, you perhaps didn't have the appropriate tools to help you regulate these emotions, which is why you kept them hidden. However, now you can learn how to be accountable and make choices that offer meaning to them. Owning these parts of your nature means expanding your existing self-definition to include more of what's actually there, and to see yourself fully.

> *It's time to reconnect to what's inside you,*
> *completing yourself with the 'good' parts as well*
> *as the 'bad' to become more whole and authentic.*

To integrate the two sides of you – your learned side and your shadow side – you need to face the shadow and learn how to regulate your emotions. This is part of your self-discovery, the path to self-awareness, and it involves digging deep to the heart of the matter. Connecting these two sides of you means opening up and understanding your internal world. It involves making the shift from outside-in to inside-out, so you no longer rely on the world around you to feel good enough; rather, you feel good enough and connect through your internal world. The change this offers your perception is so powerful.

Going Inward

So, how do you change from outside-in to inside-out? Consider that the external part of us, the one we show the world, is governed by the life rules or beliefs we've created, based on our past experiences. Although those rules/beliefs are designed to make us feel safe, they're based on fear of rejection and therefore they hold us back; we limit ourselves by trying to navigate our lives from our hidden beliefs.

If you believe you aren't good enough, it's as though you're wearing blue-tinted glasses that only let you see the world from that point of view. You'll be sensitive toward the feelings and reactions of others, not wanting to be a burden or for them to reject you in any way, and you may also struggle to take up space in situations.

Imagine you're at a friend's house for tea, and they mention they have a lot to do that evening. They may just be saying this to let you know their plans, but you might perceive it as them wanting you to leave. Why? Because you worry about being a burden or taking up space, so your blue-tinted glasses perceive this as a potential rejection. This leads you to create a story that you need to leave your friend's house, even though that's not what's been asked of you. This perception colors how you show up in life, and it affects your every interaction. Can you see how these rules we make can have an impact on how we are and what we do in the external world?

I remember an incident when I was overly mindful of someone else's time. During a training day, I wanted to ask the trainer something, but I stopped myself because I didn't want to be a burden. She'd offered space for questions, but I refused to take it up because of my self-imposed limited viewpoint at the time. When I spoke to my therapist about it afterward, we ended up delving deeper into understanding the guilt I was carrying from the story I'd told myself. I realized that I was terrified of upsetting others because my blinkered vision saw it as rejection, and I believed it.

I didn't know how to regulate rejection and instead I did everything to prevent it from potentially happening. In the process I lost myself, becoming full of self-doubt and questioning. I was very hard on myself and didn't ask for help when I needed it. This 'not good enough' internal world projected outward onto the way I showed up in the external world and how I navigated life. What I didn't realize was that this inner battle was me vs. me. Nor did I know that there were tools to overcome it.

A New Way of Being

When we gain the strength to go inward, we become more aware of the battle we have with ourselves. Initially, it can feel overwhelming because everything you think you know about yourself is changing. You're pulling all the different pieces of yourself together in order to see the bigger picture, and it's full of up-and-down emotions.

However, it's only by getting to the root cause that you can begin to negate the effects of your past beliefs and truly live a life that's free. For every effect there's a root cause. And we need to find and address the root cause rather than trying to fix the effect.

Imagine an apple tree with wilting leaves that isn't producing much blossom or fruit. You might give the tree extra water, so it perks up for a while, the leaves turning green once more and the blossom opening. But, if you don't address what's *really* wrong with the tree, this is just a temporary fix. You need to go into the soil to see which nutrients the tree may not be getting through its roots. If we focus only on reviving the leaves, we're addressing only the external issue. Sometimes we need to go deeper to see what's really going on.

It sounds like hard work. And it can be. But the rewards make it worthwhile. From this point we start to notice our intuition kicking in, answers and resolutions just 'popping' into our head in unexpected ways and at unexpected moments. Instead of using our imagination to enhance our fears, instead we harness its power to help us manifest a new way of being.

When we start to work on ourselves, we become grounded and gain clarity. We trust ourselves and use our mind constructively, so we can blossom in the most powerful and complete way.

And while we still need to feel guilt or shame when appropriate, these feelings are no longer as overpowering. Navigating our imagination is a skill we can learn. We can get better at regulating and managing our feelings, so they don't take over and dictate our behaviors.

Imagine that you're driving a car and your emotions are your passengers. One day, you take a wrong turn – that is, you do something you perceive as being wrong. In the past, shame would come and grab the wheel, taking over. Even though your other emotions are in the car as well, you never let them take the wheel, as shame is the strongest. However, once you've done the work we're looking at in this book, and have reconnected with yourself, you won't give up the wheel anymore. You'll remain in control.

Grieving for Our Old Self

You might find that you mourn the past version of you once it's gone and miss your old way of being – the identities and roles you've taken on based on this incomplete picture of who you really are. However, these must be shed in order for you to develop. Letting go of established behaviors – even when they're not satisfying – is challenging. The brain prefers familiarity and resists change. It's like a child clinging to a soothing pacifier, not wanting to let go when told it's time to do so.

While the brain may feel this is 'safe,' our rational side recognizes the need to shed old behavior patterns. Similarly, acknowledging the shadow aspects of ourselves – those we hide and deny – isn't easy. Yet, to be whole and integrated, we must confront them; otherwise, they'll persistently resurface throughout our lives. Such questioning and soul-searching can yield fruitful results. Looking deeper within also puts you in touch with positive aspects of your nature that have yet to be developed, so you can integrate them into your authentic/conscious self.

Previously, you might have developed meaning and purpose from the place of 'not good enough,' but the processes in this book will allow you to redefine your values, meaning, and purpose in life from a place of 'good enough.' As a result, you'll become more in touch with yourself than ever before and the choices and adjustments you make now are likely to be more lasting and positive. It's time to learn to relate to others in new ways, where you no longer avoid depth or commitment due to fear.

Questions for Self-Reflection

Think back to the HFA behavior types with which you identified in Step 1.

- *Do you think there's a root cause of your anxiety?*

- *What fears do you think drive some of your behaviors?*

- *What sensations do you experience in your body when you feel fear?*

Why Childhood Experiences Matter

It's been proven that our early childhood experiences can leave a lasting impression on us, buried deep within our psyche. We can carry into adulthood an underlying belief that life is unpredictable, that we're responsible for the emotions of others, and that our own feelings aren't important. We each form different beliefs about how we view ourselves, how we view others, and how we view the world. This means, therefore, that when we communicate with each other, we all come from different experiences and viewpoints.

I was a curious child and needed to understand things, but through my interactions I soon learned to dial down this part of me. As a female in my family, I was taught to nurture others. I felt that I shouldn't be a burden or 'too much' for my parents because they were busy giving me and my siblings opportunities they'd never had, and I felt guilty about deviating from the path they wanted me to take.

This pattern continued into adulthood and led to codependency. I showed up wanting to people-please and then wondered why I wasn't seen and loved in the way I wanted to be. This was quite a journey, and to me it illustrates how our experiences contribute to the formation of the beliefs and patterns we carry inside us and use to create rules about how we show up and navigate adulthood. These are what are known as 'core beliefs,' and I'll explain them more fully in the next section.

Early childhood experiences imprint on us in ways that aren't always obvious, and it's not until we have the right tools that we recognize and learn how to overcome the patterns they've left behind.

The impact of specific childhood experiences can be seen in species across the planet, not just humans. It's something deep and visceral, part of our biological makeup. Consider, for example, sea turtles. Once hatched, baby sea turtles head for the ocean, using the slope of the beach, the crests of the waves, and the light reflecting off the ocean to find their way. Those that make it to the water have a perilous journey ahead of them in a vast ocean yet, once mature, they're able to return to the exact place where they were born.

Scientists have discovered that they do this by imprinting the magnetic field of their natal beach as they take their first wobbly steps toward the ocean. They then search for this magnetic signature when they want to return 'home.' However, if a human sees a baby sea turtle struggling and tries to help it, the animal doesn't develop this specific imprint; it needs the experience of making its own way to the ocean in order to become what it's supposed to be. And it's the same for humans. We need the right conditions in which to grow and become who we're supposed to be.

Every human is unique, each with their own personality and character. Therefore, they also have unique needs, which differ from one person to another. Emotional, physical, and other forms of neglect are just like the human picking up the struggling turtle. It affects the way our brains are hardwired, leading us to develop patterns of behavior based on a belief system formed by these external experiences. We become a version of ourselves that's limited, simply because of what we believe about ourselves.

If your mother abandoned you at an early age, for example, you might form a belief or expectation that anyone you become close to or dependent on will also leave. Later, you may find yourself unconsciously drawn to those who fulfill your negative expectation, repeatedly choosing a partner who will eventually abandon you. Or you could be so frightened of someone leaving you (like your mother did) that you try to control or manipulate the relationship in a manner which ultimately drives the person away.

We behave in this way because it makes us feel safe, although what we really are is stuck. We've hidden our shadow side away – the part of us we don't want people to see. If we remain in these patterns, we'll never get to learn *why* we behave this way or be able to integrate our learned side and our shadow side.

SELF-REFLECTION

- How did you feel while you were growing up? Be honest. This isn't about pointing fingers or blaming anyone. It's about understanding your childhood.

- Break down your relationship with each parent or caregiver. What were they like? For example: *My father was emotionally distant. My mother was always there for me. My caregiver withheld love as a punishment. My caregiver was controlling.*

- Now, write down your learned inner-child belief as it relates to each relationship. For the examples above, this would be as follows: *I learned that I had to take care of myself. I learned that I was loved and supported. I learned that I had to earn love. I learned that it was easier to go along with what others wanted.*

- Do you ever remember feeling that you had to earn love? If so, what made you feel this way?

- Consider your past three relationships. Can you see a pattern in the way they played out?

Our Core Beliefs

Core beliefs are strong beliefs a person holds consistently over time that inform their worldview and self-perception. Core beliefs act as a lens through which we see the world and are generally formed early in life as a result of our childhood experiences. While they can be helpful in terms of making sense of things, they can also work against us by limiting us and preventing self-expansion.

For example, holding the core belief 'I'm not good enough' or 'Something's wrong with me' leads you to see the world through this lens. It limits you, coloring everything around you. This limited viewpoint becomes your truth – until you challenge it. You may not even be aware that you carry this core belief, yet it works beneath the surface like termites gnawing at a timber foundation, causing damage that cannot be seen. Once your unconscious mind believes something to be true, it will do anything to validate that core belief, even if it hurts you or limits you along the way.

This particular core belief can become so strong that you find yourself failing in spite of a desire to succeed. You don't understand why you keep ending up in the same patterns of behavior and these failures become a self-fulfilling prophecy, strengthening your belief that you're not good enough.

The sad part is that the core belief of not being good enough isn't true. All the work, all the damage, all the self-sabotage are the result of a bleak, negative story you've told yourself – either because of the way you've been treated in the past or because of your own self-belief. By convincing your unconscious mind that this dysfunctional story is true, you've actually *created* the reality. Your unconscious mind will act in ways you may not even notice, just to support this self-defeating truth.

It may sound as though I'm saying that this self-sabotaging behavior is your fault. That, because you've told your subconscious mind a lie that it believes is truth, you're somehow to blame. But this isn't the case. We're each shaped by our journey through life, and through our perceptions of our experiences and relationships with others.

Accepting the truth of who you are, and how your behavior has been impacted by your past, is part of the process of understanding how HFA affects you and finding the way to break free of these patterns.

> *Being kind to yourself, self-forgiveness, and being curious are all part of changing the core belief of 'I'm not good enough.'*

Layer upon Layer

The diagram below shows how our early experiences result in us forming core beliefs based around input from both our *environment* and our *genetic/neurological* makeup. These core beliefs lead us to make *assumptions* and create *life rules*, shaping how we perceive and interact with the world. While on the outside we may seem to be doing fine, anything that *triggers* a response based on these assumptions can lead to intrusive *thoughts* that are followed by *feelings, behavior,* and even *physical sensations.*

For example, the intrusive thought might be 'They don't like me,' and as a result we feel rejection; this feeling may lead to physical sensations, such as a knot in stomach, and that can lead us to shut down (the behavior). Or to go quiet and leave the room. The key is to recognize and be able to sift through these complex layers, and ultimately break free of the limiting beliefs that hold us back.

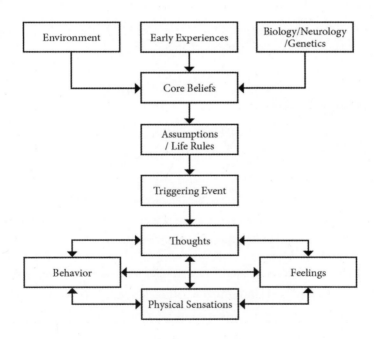

The Layers of Our Core Beliefs

But how do we change something that's been ingrained in us since childhood? The key to unlocking our true potential lies in understanding how and why these patterns were formed. While this can be difficult to pinpoint initially, there are a couple of proven psychological theories that can help us, both of which I integrate into my practice when working with clients: attachment theory and Maslow's Hierarchy of Needs.

Let's explore them both here, looking specifically at how they pertain to HFA and how you can apply them to your own experience. Once you understand the science behind HFA, we can then move on to Step 3, where you'll start using tools to help you manage it. Yes, it *is* possible to change!

Attachment Theory

It's via connection with others that we survive in this world. When we develop an attachment to another human, ultimately what we're seeking is closeness and intimacy, which is one of our primary drivers. When we're a child, our life depends on another person loving, feeding, and looking after us. Later, as an adult, we can still seek fulfillment through love and relationships.

Yet HFA, and its associated fear, can hold us back from true depth and feeling in a relationship, whether platonic, professional, or romantic. We need to understand what we give and receive in relationships, know why this is important, appreciate how we create partnerships, and go deeper into understanding intimacy.

Knowing what makes us feel secure is extraordinarily powerful because, without this understanding, when change happens it can shake our world, causing panic and anxiety. This knowledge also helps us to navigate our relationships from a place of security as opposed to fear. Here's a brief overview of attachment theory, which was developed by the British psychiatrist John Bowlby.

The Idea

Attachment theory proposes that emotional experiences early in our life can influence our later relationships, as well as our relationship with ourselves. Bowlby theorized that we come into the world biologically pre-programmed to form attachments with others, as that will help us to survive.[3] However, the *way* we form those attachments, and how we communicate with and are treated by others early in our lives, creates a template for how we experience and respond to future relationships, as well as how we feel about ourselves, how we relate to others, and our level of self-awareness.

The Understanding

When it comes to understanding how we communicate with ourselves and with others, the way that we form attachments is key. To gain deeper self-awareness, we need to go back to our early experiences. When a primary caregiver is sensitive to the needs and distress of their child and responds appropriately, the child then learns that their needs are valid and deserving of being met, leading to a positive self-image later in life. This is described as a *secure attachment*.

However, if, for whatever reason, the child's needs aren't met by their primary caregiver, then an *insecure attachment* forms. This then affects the child's future relationships in different ways. We'll look more closely at the types of secure and insecure attachment later in this section.

Attachment Theory in Action

There will always be things that challenge our relationships, especially as we continue to grow and develop. We don't stay the same and sometimes that's where the battle and difficulty lies. I describe it as like a dance where we're constantly trying to find the rhythm and flow. Sometimes we fall out of rhythm and end up trying to find that flow so we can just 'be' again.

As we experience different relationships as adults, our deep patterns and complexes rooted in childhood can still be playing out. What's key is how we work together with the other people in our lives and how we hold space to speak and communicate how we feel. We need to remember that we're on the same side rather than closing down in fear, which will stop us from being vulnerable and connecting deeply. Let's look at this using the following example of how attachment theory works in practice.

The situation: Alice's partner has planned a date night for them, and he's told her that he's organized it all. However, when the day arrives, he asks Alice what she wants to do and where she wants to eat. Alice had also asked him to buy some milk on the way home from work, but he didn't do that. Inside, Alice is so angry because she'd trusted her partner to do what he said he would. However, she doesn't want to cause conflict, so she goes out with him on the date, even though she feels frustrated and as though she hasn't been listened to or respected. She buries her resentment to avoid a potential conflict.

Attachment style: As a child, Alice had no space to share her emotions because her parent was unavailable due to working long hours. She felt that she was a burden and was being too much. Consequently, she grew up with an *insecure attachment* and was always worried about being rejected.

'Rule' in relationships: Alice learned that in order to feel needed, she had to please others in relationships. This gave her a sense of being enough.

Attachment thought process: If as a child she'd developed a *secure attachment* rather than an insecure one, Alice could have felt the following way: 'It's okay to tell my partner how it made me feel when he didn't plan the date and forgot the milk. That way he can understand why this was important for me. I'm not blaming him, but rather letting him know how I feel so we can deeply understand one another.'

This is a prime example of how our childhood experiences can inform our patterns of behavior through to adulthood. The following case study looks at this from another angle, where the attachment is formed by a child wanting not to burden their parent.

CASE STUDY

Peter grew up in a family where his mother was unwell, and his father went out to work. He remembers how difficult it was for his mother to get out of bed some days, and how consequently, he felt that he shouldn't be more of a burden for her. Whenever his mother told him she was proud of him, Peter felt happy that he was able to make her happy. Even though he struggled at school and was picked on by other children, he never told anyone as he didn't want to rock the boat or make things harder for his mother.

BEHAVIOR PATTERN

As his life went on, Peter continued to present with this pattern, including at work, in his friendships, and in his romantic relationships. He never wanted to 'rock the boat,' as he struggled when he saw others upset. This got to a point where he felt low and entered therapy to help him understand this behavior.

Through his therapy journey, Peter realized that he'd never spoken out about how he felt because he had an underlying belief that he was too much and was going to upset others. This was not a case of him blaming his parents or school for not noticing, but for him to understand how the way he experienced the world shut out his heart and allowed his brain to take control. This means that he struggled to be authentic and would scan others' reactions to help him form his own, rather than trusting his feelings. He also realized he was sensitive, and his need became focused on self-esteem instead of validation and longing for love from others.

Attachment Styles

Knowing whether you have a secure or an insecure attachment style can help you break the patterns that sabotage your relationships. It gives you awareness and understanding so you can consciously make different choices, leading to meaningful, authentic, and deeper connections.

Each of us has our own life experience to explore and our own discoveries to make. However, although your experiences are unique to you, when it comes to relationships, it's likely that you fall into one of the four main attachment styles – Insecure Anxious-Preoccupied; Insecure Dismissive-Avoidant, Insecure Fearful-Avoidant, and Secure – each of which is rooted in different childhood experiences.

A secure attachment style is associated with a positive self-image, a good capacity to manage distress, being comfortable with autonomy, and good relationship-building skills. Securely attached individuals also tend to have a greater degree of self-understanding, and therefore can convey their needs more effectively, as well as having them met.

Insecure attachment styles are characterized by negative self-perception, which can then play out later in life in several different ways. For example, an Insecure Dismissive-Avoidant person who's learned that their needs won't be met, will go on to demonstrate low levels of affection and avoid close relationships. However, an Insecure Anxious-Preoccupied person will actually increase their levels of distress in order to have their needs met, leading to drama in their relationships later in life.

Attachment Type	Description	Behavioral Traits	Rooted Experience
Insecure Anxious-Preoccupied	Seek high levels of intimacy, approval, and responsiveness from their partners.	May worry about their partner's love and have heightened sensitivity to any perceived threat to the relationship.	An initial attachment where affection felt conditional, such as a caregiver who withheld love as punishment.
Insecure Dismissive-Avoidant	Tend to distance themselves emotionally from others and may avoid intimate relationships.	May prioritize independence, suppress their emotions, and have difficulty relying on others.	An initial attachment which may have involved neglect or other forms of abuse.
Insecure Fearful-Avoidant or Disorganized	A mix of anxious and avoidant traits. They desire closeness but may also fear rejection.	May have difficulty trusting others, struggle with self-worth, and exhibit erratic behaviors in relationships.	An initial attachment where the caregiver was unreliable and/or inconsistent, in terms of care, punishment, and affection.
Secure	Feel comfortable with emotional intimacy and are generally secure in themselves and their relationships.	Can trust others, feel safe exploring the world, and are effective in managing stress.	An initial attachment where the caregiver could be relied upon, was consistent and also affectionate.

An Overview of the Four Attachment Styles

WHAT'S YOUR ATTACHMENT STYLE?

This quiz is an informal way to self-assess, gain insight, and help you identify your attachment style. Attachment styles are complex and influenced by various factors, so this offers a general sense of your primary attachment tendencies rather than a definitive diagnosis.

When considering the questions below, think about your personal, professional, *and* romantic relationships where appropriate.

1. How comfortable are you with closeness and intimacy in relationships?

    a. Very comfortable. I find it easy to open up, get close to others, and connect emotionally.

    b. Somewhat comfortable, but it takes time for me to trust and open up to others.

    c. Uncomfortable. I prefer independence and have difficulty opening up in close relationships.

2. How do you usually respond to conflict or arguments in relationships?

    a. I try to seek resolution and communicate openly to resolve issues.

    b. I try to compromise and find a middle ground but might avoid conflict to maintain harmony.

    c. I tend to withdraw or distance myself when conflicts arise.

3. Do you often worry about being abandoned or left alone in relationships?

    a. No, I feel secure and confident in my relationships.

    b. Sometimes, especially when there are signs of tension or conflict in the relationship.

    c. Yes, I frequently fear abandonment and often feel insecure in relationships.

4. How comfortable are you with depending on others or letting others depend on you?

    a. I'm comfortable both depending on others and letting others depend on me.

b. I prefer some level of independence but can rely on others when needed.

c. I find it hard to depend on others or to let others get too close to me.

5. Can you easily trust others and believe they have your best interests at heart?

a. Yes, I generally trust people and believe they mean well.

b. I trust cautiously and take time to build trust in others.

c. No, I find it hard to trust others and often feel like I'll be let down.

Scoring: Count how many (a), (b), and (c) answers you selected:

- If you scored mostly (a) answers, this suggests you have a secure attachment style.

- If you scored mostly (b) answers, this suggests you have an anxious-preoccupied attachment style.

- If you scored mostly (c) answers, this suggests you have a dismissive-avoidant attachment style.

Remember, this quiz is intended for self-reflection and may not fully capture the complexity of attachment styles. It's advisable to seek the help of a mental health professional for a more accurate and comprehensive assessment if needed.

However, whatever quiz result you have now, it doesn't mean it will always be this way. This is part of the understanding that will lead to change. Realizing that the way you act in a relationship is based on how you were treated in the past is a step toward choosing a different way of being.

Questions for Self-Reflection

- *Now that you know your attachment style, can you look back at your early experiences and see where this might have come from?*

- *How does your attachment style shape the relationships you currently hold, whether platonic, business, or romantic?*

- *What choices, if any, can you make to break free of these patterns?*

- *What does a healthy relationship look like to you?*

Maslow's Hierarchy of Needs

When HFA is discussed, the word *need* comes up quite often. This is because we learn self-defeating patterns of behavior in order to satisfy the needs we've developed as a result of our past experiences. By completing the quiz above, you've determined which attachment style you embody, so now let's talk more about need.

One of the most popular theories of need was developed by US psychologist Abraham Maslow, who believed that, as humans, we're all striving toward what he called 'self-actualization,' which is another way of saying 'the best version of ourselves.' To reach self-actualization, Maslow said, we must first meet the different 'levels' of human need.[4]

When we have HFA, we're always trying to meet our unspoken needs based on our learned experiences, which manifest in the patterns of behavior we present, the space we take up, and the unconscious rules by which we live. However, if these patterns depend on other people behaving in a certain way in order to meet *our* needs, they'll become difficult and exhausting to maintain. Looking externally to meet our needs means we'll never reach self-actualization – to get there, we must go inward.

The Idea

Building on the work done on attachment theory by John Bowlby, Maslow came up with what he called the Hierarchy of Needs. The Hierarchy of Needs is often depicted as a five-level pyramid (see the diagram opposite), with the needs ordered in accordance with their importance: the first level is our basic physiological needs (such as air, water, food, shelter, and sleep); the second level is to do with safety and security; the third level is love and belonging; the fourth level is esteem (of the self and by others); and the final level is self-actualization – a need for personal growth and discovery, of being the best a person can be, which is unique to every individual.

The Understanding

As you can see in the diagram, these levels of need follow one to the next. However, we can achieve one level without necessarily fulfilling the previous level, and achieving all the levels doesn't necessarily mean we'll reach self-actualization; Maslow didn't believe that satisfying the first four levels automatically led to the fifth. Meeting the needs on each level of the pyramid may come easier to some; for example, being safe, having enough to eat, or experiencing sexual intimacy is out of reach for some people. However, it doesn't mean that self-actualization is also out of reach.

Maslow's Hierarchy of Needs

Maslow theorized that personal growth is an ongoing process and that we're always evolving, growing, and changing; it's through communication with others that we're able to enhance ourselves and keep the pace of growth flourishing. This growth is in constant development because it involves our unique talents, capacities, and potentialities. When we broaden our perspective and engage in challenging experiences – learning new skills and testing ourselves in unfamiliar territories – we continue to grow.

Our Needs and HFA-Related Perfectionism

Low self-esteem may hold us back from the higher levels within the pyramid – once again tying in with HFA and the feeling of not being good enough. Let's take a look at how Maslow's Hierarchy of Needs relates to HFA through its associated behavior of perfectionism.

Physiological Needs

High-functioning anxiety and perfectionism can create a hyperfocus on achievement and success, as we prioritize meeting self-imposed high standards. Constantly pushing ourselves to excel and meet unrealistic standards may result in sleep disturbances, irregular eating patterns, and chronic stress. Over time, this can negatively impact our physical health and overall well-being.

Safety Needs

Perfectionists may rely heavily on external validation to feel safe and secure. HFA intensifies this need for certainty, leading to hypervigilance and a constant fear of failure. The fear of not living up to expectations or making mistakes can lead to chronic anxiety, hindering our sense of safety and preventing us from embracing uncertainty.

Love and Belonging Needs

Striving for perfection and constantly seeking approval or acceptance from others may make it difficult for us to form authentic connections and relationships, as we may fear judgment or rejection if we don't meet our own or others' expectations. This fear of not being accepted for who we truly are can prevent us from experiencing genuine love and belongingness.

Esteem Needs

While perfectionists may receive external recognition and praise, their self-esteem is often contingent on meeting impossibly high standards. HFA can magnify feelings of self-doubt and inadequacy, leading to a perpetual feeling of inadequacy, and even imposter syndrome.

Self-Actualization

HFA and perfectionism can hinder self-actualization, the process of reaching our full potential and pursuing personal growth and fulfillment. The constant pursuit of perfection and our self-criticism and fear of failure may prevent us from taking risks and exploring our true passions and interests, limiting our opportunities for self-discovery and growth.

Toward Authenticity

In summary, HFA and perfectionism can disrupt the balance of Maslow's Hierarchy of Needs, preventing us from fully satisfying our lower-level needs and hindering our progress toward self-actualization. But by nurturing a healthy sense of self-worth and reframing perfectionism, we can better align with our needs and find fulfillment in authentic connections, free from the burdens of anxiety and the pursuit of unattainable perfection.

Addressing and managing this involves recognizing the impact of anxiety and perfectionism and taking proactive steps to cultivate self-compassion, set realistic expectations, and seek support when needed. By addressing these underlying issues, we can then foster personal growth and well-being, ultimately moving toward self-actualization and a more balanced and fulfilling life.

> *It's via interaction with others that we understand not only who we are but also who we can be. Every interaction brings the possibility of learning something new.*

Why? Because it may bring something to our inner world or it may feel good, or even challenging. Whatever the situation, the learning adds to both our wisdom and understanding of how we want to show up in the future.

If you have low self-esteem, it can feel like you're stuck when it comes to finding lasting love and feeling as though you belong, because you develop your self-worth through needing to be liked by others. Not having a positive external relationship base in early life can hinder the development of self-esteem.

For example, if every time you cried as a child, your caregiver told you to stop because only babies cry, it could have made you feel that crying wasn't allowed. They may have thought they were soothing you but instead it instilled in you a negative belief, leading you to smile when you really want to cry simply to get the praise you crave. You grew up seeking this validation from others, as it's the only way you know to prove that you're enough. You've learned that you can't make decisions for yourself and that you need others to show you the way.

However, when you step back and look at this learned behavior, and understand where it came from, it becomes clear that this is your *perception* of what others think of you rather than what they actually think.

In my own work I use a three-level model called the Pyramid of Self-Worth. The first level is self-awareness, which is where we become aware of our true self and what we truly desire. The second level is self-acceptance, where we accept this true self, embracing all that it has to offer. And the third level is self-love, where we move past acceptance to truly loving ourselves and all that we are – when we know that we're enough.

We blossom differently when we know that we're enough. I call this self-expansion – when you let go of what doesn't serve you to let in what fulfills you. Truly examining all aspects of our behavior and where it comes from allows us to lose our old beliefs about who we think we are and embrace everything that we can be.

While many of us may not achieve our full potential, Maslow believed that every single one of us has what he called 'peak achievements,' moments of self-actualization where we achieve things that we never thought possible and for which we've worked hard – such as completing a degree, running a marathon, creating a work of art, or other significant life events.[5]

Questions for Self-Reflection

- *Which level of Maslow's pyramid do you feel you're showing up as right now? Let's go deeper and get curious about it – why?*

- *What do you need to give yourself in order to rise further up the pyramid?*

- *Have you ever had a 'peak experience'? And if so, are you proud of what you achieved? If not, why is that?*

People-Pleasing Behavior

Emotional neglect early in life can lead to behaviors such as people-pleasing, being over-responsible, wanting to feel in control, and other symptoms of HFA (see Step 1). It becomes apparent that, if our emotional requirements aren't met in the way we need them to be, then we'll find other ways to feed this need, which can then lead to HFA. The good news is that once we understand this, we can make conscious decisions to change our behavior patterns. Here's a case study that demonstrates how this can be done.

CASE STUDY

As a child, Michael lived in a household where his physical needs, such as warm clothes and a safe environment, were met but his emotional safety needs were not. His parents divorced when he was eight years old, and he remembers them fighting, and his mother telling him that his father had been unfair.

When Michael grew up, he took on the role of the 'responsible one' in his relationships, including those at work, where he was seen as a good leader. He met his need to feel loved and to belong by managing everyone else's feelings and making sure they were all right.

BEHAVIOR PATTERN

When Michael was a child and his mother was upset, he didn't want to make things worse for her. Therefore, he tried to give her what he felt she needed in order to prevent her becoming more unhappy. He felt responsible for his mother's feelings and, as a result, he chose to not spend time with his father so as not to hurt her. This pattern of behavior continued into adulthood, with Michael trying to prove that he was good enough by being responsible for everyone else.

UNDERSTANDING

Only when Michael started to recognize this pattern could he break free from it. With this increased self-awareness came self-esteem, fostering a deeper understanding, acceptance, and appreciation of his authentic self. He began to understand he could feel good enough without needing to please others. He also learned that he couldn't 'fix' things for everyone, and he had to adapt to being comfortable with this. He developed confidence, boundaries, and respect for others and became more intentional, meaningful, and conscious with his decisions in life.

At this point, I'd like to remind you that this and all the case studies I share with you are intended as examples. Everyone's experience is unique and is based on their upbringing and other contributing factors. So, while these stories may resonate with you on some level, it's important to explore your own experience to truly discover how this applies to you. It's also important to note that different people may respond differently to the same stimulus or experience.

People-pleasing isn't about being caring and wanting other people to be happy; it's about organizing the reactions of other people in order to feel safe. At its core, people-pleasing is about fear of rejection or being disliked – or disliking ourselves. We spend our lives pleasing other people, saying 'yes' to accommodate their needs without understanding or even contemplating the alternative of saying 'no'. In fact, there are two sides to being a people-pleaser, as this table shows:

Learned Side (What We Show)	Shadow Side (What We Hide)
Motivated	Self-critical
Helpful	Seeks validation
Productive	Negative self-image
Organized	Disconnected
Reliable	Low self-worth
Polite	Resentful
Attentive	Lonely
Understanding	Lacks boundaries
Caring	Anxious
Loyal	Burned-out
Contented	Lost

The Two Sides of People-Pleasing Behavior

Become a Reformed People-Pleaser

A reformed people-pleaser is an individual who has consciously and intentionally worked to break free from the pattern of constantly seeking approval and prioritizing others' needs over their own. They have undergone a process of self-discovery, boundary setting, and learning to assert themselves authentically, cultivating a healthier balance between meeting their own needs and accommodating others.

LEARN TO SAY 'NO'

How often do you say 'yes' when you really want to say 'no'? Grab a coffee and a pen and paper, then find a quiet place to complete this people-pleaser exercise – it will help you establish when you need to say 'no.'

- Draw a circle and give it the heading 'time.' Now, using the categories sleep, work, travel, social, me time, family, and friends, carve the circle up into segments that represent how you *currently* spend your time, on average, over a month. *Be honest.*

- Draw a second circle and head it 'time.' Now, using the same categories, carve the circle into segments that represent how you would ideally like to spend your time.

- Draw a third circle and label it 'relationships.' Now carve it into segments for the people you currently spend your time with, using categories like me, my partner, kids, family (those I like), family (those I don't like), colleagues (like), colleagues (don't like), friends (like), friends (don't like), clients (like), clients (don't like).

- Draw a fourth circle and label it 'relationships.' Now create segments for the people you would ideally like to spend your time with.

- Next, with circles one to four in mind, compile a list that will identify (1) occasions when you're saying 'yes' when you want or need to say 'no' *or* (2) people you're spending time with and don't want to. Be brutally honest here.

- Now bring in a close (sensible) friend or spouse who you trust to help you. Then go through the list and ask yourself, *Do I have a choice in this matter?* If you do have a choice (and nine times out of 10 you will), *stop doing that thing or seeing that person.* It's really that simple.

- Rehearse what needs to be said and politely say it. If necessary, write a letter or an email. Where you can, explain your reasons. If you don't have a realistic choice in the matter (due to family obligations, work colleagues, or an event), brainstorm options as to how you can lessen the impact of that thing/person on your life. *Take action.*

Your new stance may shock or offend people, so anticipate how you want to handle this in advance. But stand firm. This is not a debate. You don't need anyone's permission. This is about making your life happier. As I always say, life's too short to be living it any other way but happy. So don't fill up your days doing things or seeing people you don't want to.

Waking Up to the Real You

While knowing your attachment style or seeing where you are on the Hierarchy of Needs pyramid won't *immediately* help your situation, it can assist you in gaining awareness, which can then be used to break the destructive patterns of behavior that are holding you back. As I mentioned earlier, it's by understanding these patterns that we're able to overcome them and finally move on from the childhood events that have subconsciously shaped us.

While our past may have defined us, it's in our present that we can let go of expectations, connect with ourselves, and re-learn how to be.

Of course, our conscious mind may refuse to do this. It's not always easy to recognize or acknowledge what needs to be changed in our lives, and there can be an overwhelming desire to stay in the 'comfort zone' of established behavioral patterns. But life may force us to change, whether through crisis or breakdown or simply being tired of living the way we do.

Although you may not feel at the time that the work you're doing on yourself is valuable or positive, with awareness comes insight, followed by illumination and self-expansion. This then leads to renewal and transformation that you may never have thought possible, removing obstacles which hold you back from further growth and development.

I share with my clients the tools they need to understand *why* they do the things they do – the same tools I'm sharing with you in this book. This helps them gain the insight they need to break free of these behavior patterns. Many clients tell me they wish they'd gone through this process of 'waking up' earlier in their lives, and how frustrated and cheated they feel that they continued these patterns.

They reflect on the fact they've been stuck living for others because of their own limiting core beliefs, and on how breaking free of them has made them realize they had their head in the sand for years, not knowing there was a different way to do things. But it's not their fault. Just as the sea turtle may not realize its brain has been rewired by the (un)helpful human, so it is for us, too.

When I reflect on my life, I feel grief about the path I've walked. I remember how, after being diagnosed with dyslexia, I started to understand why I revised the way I did, and why I struggled to read. I remember one occasion when a teacher picked me to read a few pages of a book. I was struck by anxiety and panic on the inside, yet I found a way to get through. There were words I found difficult to pronounce (I still do) and I could hear other students laughing. Inside I was full of shame, but I kept going despite them. I can see now why my teachers hadn't noticed what was going on, as I'd learned not to show how I was feeling. This, to me, is a prime example of the two-sided behavior of HFA. Can you relate to this?

SELF-REFLECTION

Write down five words that describe your childhood. For example: challenging, supportive, adventurous, caring, confusing.

- Which of these words would you say have carried over into your adult life?

- Which of these words would you like to change? For example: 'supportive' and 'caring' both shape the way I seek and offer support in relationships. 'Adventurous' influences my openness to new experiences and challenges. 'Confusing' reflects how I can often shut down as a result of not understanding someone else's perspective.

- What insight about your patterns of behavior can you gain from these words?

The Path to Self-Awareness

Self-awareness is about learning to better understand why you feel what you feel, think what you think, and why you behave in a particular way. It's also a reflection of how you see yourself and it can relate to personal development. This growing awareness of one's stance in the world is integral to developing secure relationships.

There's still so much we don't know about what happens in our subconscious mind, but what is clear is how important our subconscious is in terms of influencing our behavior.

> *Only by giving ourselves the space to pause*
> *and become conscious can we gain insight*
> *into how we present ourselves.*

Otherwise, the patterns imprinted on our subconscious when we were young will remain in place, keeping us on an autopilot loop, even if our situation changes.

There's a story about captive elephants that were tied with chains when they were babies to teach them that they couldn't escape. When they were older, the chains were changed to ropes, which the now-strong elephants could easily break and free themselves. Yet they didn't, because they still believed they were in chains. The belief that they couldn't escape was imprinted on them when they were young and it remained, as strong as the chains that once bound them.

This rather sad story shows us how easily we can be caught up in our own metaphorical chains, simply because of things we experienced when we were young that are still with us. Our mind is trained to keep us safe, and it does so by installing behaviors that protect us from experiencing the feeling of not being good enough that we learned as a child. But these behaviors gradually become like chains, holding us back from living life to the full. Only through increased self-awareness can we start to break free.

If, for example, as a child your mother repeatedly pushed you away when you reached out for her, you'll have formed certain opinions or beliefs about yourself, others, and the world based on that experience. You might think you're unlovable and unworthy and believe that whenever you ask for something you need, you'll be rejected. You might have learned that you can't trust other people or rely on them. You may have got used to handling things alone and learned that you must depend on yourself.

However, these feelings cannot stay hidden forever – they'll emerge as frustration, resentment, or anger at some time in your life, when someone doesn't meet your expectations. You're bound by the memory of your past and, unless you understand that the chains are no longer there, you're never going to break free.

Questions for Self-Reflection

- *When are you most critical of yourself? For example, at work, in a relationship, when out in public, at home alone.*

- *Are there situations where you pretend to be someone you're not in order to gain acceptance from others?*

- *Are there particular people around whom you feel more sensitive/uncomfortable? Do they have anything in common?*

- *When do you feel that your sense of self-worth increases?*

- *What judgment from others do you fear the most?*

- *Do you feel you hold a belief that holds you back?*

- *Can you recall an early experience of rejection?*

Taking Stock

Now that you've almost completed Step 2, how do you feel? Take a moment to let everything you might have learned about yourself sink in. And also give yourself a pat on the back. By simply getting to this point – by holding this book in your hands and being engaged and curious enough to keep going – you've demonstrated your inner courage and strength.

You hold the key to releasing your limiting beliefs and behavior, and breaking free rather than remaining stuck. Be proud of yourself for all that you've achieved so far, and for wanting to go deeper and understand. The journey to our own core is one that can be difficult and fraught with emotion at times. Reconciling the learned and shadow sides of ourselves isn't easy. But the rewards are there if you're strong enough to keep going. And I believe that you are.

STEP 2 SUMMARY

I hope you now have a better understanding of where HFA come from, and how, once we understand the *origins* of the patterns of behavior associated with it, we can begin to *unlearn* them. Take the opportunity now to explore more fully the inner images and patterns you've harbored since childhood and see how these show up as HFA and not feeling good enough. The understanding you'll gain from doing so will generate new insights in your subconscious, bringing them into the light. Remember, when you give yourself the time and space to make things conscious, powerful things can happen.

This is the time to change. You may have spent a lot of your life doing what you think others think you should be doing. Now you have the opportunity to pause, reflect, and take stock. Through evaluating, reflecting on, and processing what you've accomplished or not accomplished so far, you'll be able to reassess and reformulate the values, goals, and objectives that are important to you now. Reconsider what's personally meaningful to you. What are your personal needs and desires? What's the purpose of your existence? What do you want to do with the years you have left?

It's possible to clear the old to make way for the new. It's time to give yourself permission to be who you are – to do what you want to do, not just what you *think* you should be doing. The *unlearning* is now complete, and it's time for the *learning* to begin. In the next three steps I'll give you the tools you need to enter a new state of being. Are you ready?

Learn -ing

STEP 3

Develop Self-Connection and Transcend Your Fear

Me: (Therapist) You said that you don't want to do this presentation for work.

Client: *Yes. I don't feel comfortable.*

Me: What do you mean by comfortable?

Client: *People expect me to speak about this topic and know everything, and I don't.*

Me: What would happen if you said something that someone didn't agree with?

Client: *People would judge me and think I was stupid.*

Me: So, you're worried about what people might think of you if you were to get something 'wrong'?

Client: *Yes, because they wouldn't accept me.*

Me: So, you're fearful of being rejected by others?

Client: *I didn't think of it like that, but yes – I don't want to come across as not good enough.*

The path to self-awareness, to knowing and accepting who we really are, is one that can take time to travel. However, if you've been doing the work so far, you're already on your way. So, let's take a moment to pause. I know, you're probably thinking: *But I've just learned about why I feel the way I do, and where it came from. I've dug deep, made contact with parts of me I thought were hidden away forever. I've peeled back lots of layers and exposed a lot of fear. And now you want me to... pause?*

Well, not exactly. This is the place on our journey together where we take stock of what we've discovered. Where we seek clarity. HFA, as I've previously stated, comes from a place of fear. In Steps 1 and 2 you did some work to discover where your fear comes from, releasing it into the light. Now, before you move on, you need to *understand* your fear. Only then can you move forward and be truly free.

> **When we become clear about what our fear is trying to tell us, we can unlearn our existing way of being and learn a new way.**

The people I work with often say to me, 'But I don't know who I am if I stop being this way.' Accepting this is a big part of letting go of the fear. Who are you when fear isn't driving you?

Making Sense of Our Behavior Patterns

In Step 2 we went back into the past to discover how HFA can develop as a result of our childhood experiences. We explored our core beliefs, the four attachment styles, and the idea of need, and we looked at how our experiences when young follow us into adulthood. This was *unlearning*.

I used the analogy of an archaeologist digging through layers to get to the past. However, once the archaeologist reaches the bottom of the trench, they need to examine each of those layers, sifting through the soil to extract every grain of learning. And it's the same for us in this process of discovery. While we now know where these behavior patterns come from, the work lies in understanding them. This is the first step in *learning* a new way of being.

During infancy, our life depends on the people who look after us and provide for our needs. Should our caregivers not meet our physical, emotional, and safety needs, later we'll find other ways (unconsciously) to meet them. We can also be angry with our caregivers for not supporting us, feel as though they let us down, or feel guilty for being a burden or asking for too much.

We're doomed to relive these childhood beliefs, patterns, and expectations until we bring them into our consciousness and make sense of them. Until we can give a different meaning to the events that occurred.

You've already done the hardest part of this process, which is acknowledging your shadow side and the patterns that show up in your life. Now it's time to dig deeper and equip yourself with the tools you need to help you navigate life moving forward. When we look objectively at our behavior patterns and rules for life, we can better understand how they were formed. We can liberate ourselves from repeating the same behaviors over and over again.

Bringing your patterns and rules for life into the light and exploring their origins is the first step toward gaining your freedom and inner peace.

The body has its own memory, and it stores feelings within. When we shut down our rage at our caregivers for not being able to give us what we need, channeling it into behavior that limits us, we also disconnect from the power inside us. By going back into our past, into our early anger and pain, we can free this trapped and suppressed energy, reintegrating it into our psyche and reinvigorating both our body and mind.

Understanding our patterns will help us find the power within us to direct our lives. As we dig deep, we'll discover an inner strength and sense of independence that will help us to gain a new direction or purpose.

It all sounds wonderful, and it can be. But getting to this point is a process and along the way it can feel like our foundations are being rocked beneath us, as if in an earthquake. This is because, even if the old structures in our life haven't been satisfying, we can still find it difficult to let go of what's familiar and established. We cling to the known and existing, even though another part wants to break free.

We see necessary change as a threat to our existence, as these old structures, or behavior patterns, have provided us with our greatest sense of security or safety. So, even as outside events might force us to face up to ourselves, we continue to hold on to old ways of being, hoping that the shaking might stop, even as the structures in our life collapse. This upheaval, difficult as it might seem at the time, is a necessary part of letting go, and it's happening for a reason. We're tapping into our 'core self' and taking back our power.

Reconnecting with Our Core Self

There are many who believe that we all have a deeper, or core, self, which operates from the subconscious mind to guide us and regulate our growth and development. Just as a pear seed knows that it's meant to grow into a pear tree and not an apple tree, there's a part of us which knows what we're meant to become, and the path we need to take to get there. When people talk about 'trusting their gut,' they may be tapping into this deep part of us. However, trust is difficult for people with HFA, so they lose that connection with their core self.

Through learning to trust ourselves, sitting in stillness and being guided toward peace, we can reconnect with our core self and find ourselves again. Concepts such as individualization, self-realization, self-fulfillment, and awakening all describe this process of growing into what we're meant to become, using wisdom and meaning taken from all that we've been through. We can grow through what we've experienced.

Even if we don't believe in the concept of a deeper self guiding us, finding meaning in our situation makes it easier to deal with it more creatively and successfully. We need to let the earthquake have its way, let it break down what was old and limiting in order to make way for building something new. It's the only way to access the power inside.

> *Once we reconnect to our inner power, our core self, we feel not only more whole but more alive, connected, and grounded. It's so beautiful.*

We feel empowered to make decisions and get to a point where we trust we'll be okay, even in situations that previously would have overwhelmed or frightened us. Starting this process is like digging down even deeper to reclaim unexpressed positive traits we've hidden away and have been unable to access, like jewels lost in the soil.

It's time now to use what you've learned (and unlearned) in Steps 1 and 2 and make the choice to show up in a different way. As you get to the root of your HFA, you can finally understand where it comes from and how it's been influencing you and your behavior.

Remember, HFA is rooted in fear. The secret to overcoming this is to learn how to manage the fear – how to dance with it rather than letting it take over. But you can only do this once you understand what the fear is trying to tell you, and this will be different for every one of us. Only by reconnecting with your core self can you release and build a different way of being.

The HFA Tool Kit

There are no hard-and-fast rules that will give you the key to changing your life. We're all unique, and what might work for one person may not work for another. Change is about you trying different things to see if they work for you. What I can do, however, is give you the tools to start the work.

So, try out each of the following HFA tools and see what feels right for you. And remember to be gentle with yourself! You're unlearning and changing years of being, which will take time. So have faith that you'll get there.

If you're a *Star Wars* fan, you might get the following analogy (if not, move on to Tool 1). When a student is training to be a Jedi Master, they ask Yoda what they need to do. His famous response is, 'Patience you must have, my young Padawan.' Becoming a Jedi requires an ability to turn down the volume on everything in your immediate surroundings, so that you can channel and feel the force. This is the thing that we need to do – be in the moment so we can regulate our emotions.

Tool 1: Let Go of Expectations

At some point in my life, I got tired of all the disappointments and heartbreak because *what I expected* didn't come to fruition. After a lot of reflection and hard work, I now try my absolute best not to have expectations. I try to let things be, and let the pieces fall where they will. Following this 'strategy' or way of life has made me more at peace and accepting of life, events, and myself. Sure,

I still want to slap myself when I have an expectation (a pesky habit that's hard to shake 100 percent), but I'm unlearning years of conditions that I lived by.

An expectation is a want, desire, belief, or emotional anticipation you have about a *future* vision of yourself, an event, or action. Expectations can be realistic or unrealistic, and it's usually the unrealistic expectations that cause us hurt, suffering, and frustration. It's essential to be aware that not all expectations are bad. It's the too-high expectations that catch us out, setting us up for failure.

When we expect things, we believe that *something will happen* in one way. But things don't always go according to plan, or you may have expected more than was realistically possible. When our expectation doesn't become reality, we feel disappointment and, eventually, even resentment. In fact, the power of unmet expectations is *so* significant that it negatively impacts how we see ourselves, the people around us, and the world.

CASE STUDY

Diane has a friend who she hasn't seen in ages. The friend contacts Diane, telling her that she's coming to town to celebrate her birthday and has arranged an evening out. Diane's excited, anticipating that her friend has booked somewhere nice for them to go. But when Diane finally meets up with her friend, she asks her, 'What do you want to do?'

Diane experiences frustration because, based on what her friend had said, she'd expected everything to already be arranged. This situation triggers Diane to feel as though she's not good enough, and as though she doesn't matter. She feels disappointed and stupid, berating herself for even thinking her friend was going to organize something for her birthday.

> **The CHILD who grows up feeling anxious and uncertain about feeling lovable = the ADULT who has high expectations of self and others.**

Letting go of your expectations requires you to spend some time with yourself. It requires honesty, and the willingness to open up. While the pathway to getting there might be different for everyone, one exercise that could be useful is to sit and breathe.

INTENTIONAL BREATHING REFLECTION

Find a quiet space where you won't be interrupted and set a timer for a duration that suits you, whether it's five minutes, 10 minutes, or longer. Even a few moments can have a meaningful impact.

- Get into a comfortable seated position and bring your focus to your breath. Imagine waves gently rolling in and out on the shore. Sync your breath with this rhythmic image, allowing any thoughts to rise and fall like the waves. Observe each thought, then let it gracefully drift away with the tide.

- Reflect on this question: Who am I in this moment? Consider who you aspire to be. Allow the answers to surface naturally; don't force them. It might be difficult at first, and you may only last a minute, but keep going. There's no right or wrong amount of time. Transformation is a marathon, not a sprint.

Whenever you want to change something, you need to first acknowledge that it exists and that it's a problem. The first step in letting go of your expectations is to realize that you *have* expectations, and then identify what they are.

Questions for Self-Reflection

- *What are your expectations of yourself?*

- *What do you expect of others? (Write down individual names if you wish.)*

- *What are your expectations regarding events in your life, your future dreams, and the world in general? How do you feel when you don't get these things?*

Tool 2: Reconnect with Your Heart's Desire

In order to courageously open our hearts again, we need to cut the cord of wanting others to validate whether or not we're good enough. The thing that connects what we truly desire with what we actually show others is a fear of being judged and found wanting; this leads to rejection and a feeling of not being good enough.

CASE STUDY

Shane's grown up feeling as if he's too much. He's also over-responsible and struggles whenever there's any sort of conflict. In his relationships, he gets to the point where he's finally comfortable with his partner and feels that they understand him; however, when he opens up and is intimate with them, letting himself be vulnerable and sharing a side of himself that he doesn't usually share, they tell him that they don't want to be with him anymore, as they don't see the relationship working out.

Shane then feels so ashamed and blames himself. He goes back into his shell, hiding himself away and locking up his pain at not feeling enough. He tells himself he's never going to allow himself to be vulnerable with anyone again because he doesn't want to feel the rejection that he's just felt.

> **The CHILD who grew up feeling he's too much
> = the ADULT who worries about what others
> think of him and fears rejection.**

It's only when we overcome that fear that we allow ourselves to be vulnerable, because then we trust ourselves and truly believe we're good enough without needing the validation of others. While we can't control how other people behave toward us, we know we have our own back and can express what it is we truly want. We may need to pause and reflect to get there, but we trust that we're okay.

Questions for Self-Reflection

Take the self-reflection questions below and either write them down on a piece of paper or read them out to yourself. Next, take a moment to truly consider your response to each one. It might take more than one attempt to get to the heart of what it is you truly desire.

Be honest. There's no space for fear in this exercise or worry about what others might think of you. It's between you and the piece of paper, so don't hold back. These questions can be about any kind of relationship in your life, not just romantic ones.

- *What is it that your heart desires? What do you long for?*

- *What behaviors have you developed to get your needs met, even in the smallest way?*

- *What makes you feel loved?*

- *What's stopping you from letting people know what you need/want?*

- *If fear wasn't there, how would you truly want to be loved by another? How would someone show up, loving you?*

- *What is it that you really want from another person (whether family, friend, or romantic relationship)?*

- *We all strive to be wanted by others. How is it that you want to be wanted?*

- *Are you worried about being vulnerable? Why? Is it because you worry about being rejected? Do you feel you'll be 'too much'? Where did you hear you are too much?*

Tool 3: Make Friends with Your Fear

Fear is like the elephant in the room. We know it's there, but we choose to ignore it because we worry about what could happen if we acknowledge its presence. We all have a different relationship with our fear, but we can't keep avoiding it. The best way forward, as is often the case in life, is to make friends with it.

Perhaps now you're thinking, *Lalitaa, what's going on? You want me to befriend my fear when I've spent my entire life avoiding it and constructing ways to feel safe?* Yes, that's exactly what I want you to do. The elephant might be huge and scary, but it's in the room with you and it's not going anywhere. You can keep trying to avoid it and ignore it, but it will still be there. You can't run away from it.

Remember in Step 1, where we talked about the double-sided behavior of HFA and how it affects us? How we show the world what we think it wants to see, and behave in ways that make us feel safe, all the while denying or avoiding what we really want and who we really are? *That's* the elephant. When you have HFA, it's not just in the room with you, it's inside you.

CASE STUDY

Joyce has a friend who often calls her to talk about her relationship difficulties. Joyce struggles to not take her friend's calls because she worries about upsetting her. So, Joyce picks up, even though it stops her from doing what she wants/needs to do. Because of her worry, Joyce makes herself available, even though it's detrimental to her.

Joyce is answering the calls because she'd rather do that than face the elephant in the room, which is her fear of angering her friend by not being available. She's afraid of not being needed, and afraid that she might lose her friend by not being good enough or constantly available to chat. But if Joyce 'makes friends' with her elephant, she'll learn that it's okay to set a boundary without feeling guilty. It's okay for her not to answer a call, or to let her friend know she's unavailable. It's okay for Joyce to put herself first. And if her friend is a good friend, she'll understand this.

The CHILD who learned to feel guilty if she upset others = the ADULT who worries about letting other people down.

Making friends with your fear might seem an impossible task. However, when you consider that friendship often comes from understanding, the path becomes a little clearer. First, work out why you're frightened: is it rejection you fear, or what other people might think of you, or things going wrong? Break it down into parts. Where does that fear truly come from?

Once you understand your fear, choose to sit with it and embrace it instead of running away. Trust me, once you make friends with it, you'll say to yourself, *Why was I running away from this?* It's challenging to make friends with your fear if you've never done it before and it can feel overwhelming at first; however, the more you do it, the easier it becomes. After all, fear is a mechanism the brain uses to keep us safe. The key is to understand fear enough that you know when to listen and when to step away from it. Once you understand where your fear comes from, you'll be able to find your own way to manage it, and the elephant will become your friend.

Questions for Self-Reflection

If you're honest with yourself about which fear you're avoiding, ask yourself the following questions:

- *What does the fear say is the worst thing that can happen?*

- *How do you feel this fear holds you back?*

- *Why do you think you haven't addressed the fear?*

Tool 4: Reflect on Your Unspoken Words

People with HFA tend to hold back on what they really want to say, either because of a fear of what others might think of them or because they learned, when younger, that their needs/thoughts weren't worth being shared as they were rarely met.

Of course, we can't all go around constantly speaking our mind, unless we want to offend everyone. Tact and manners are concepts for a reason. However, the unspoken words I'm referring to are the ones we're frightened to share, for whatever reason. It's important to face up to these words, to listen to them properly, even if no one else does. To acknowledge that they exist so we can move past the fear that's holding us back.

When we think of fear, we need to understand what it actually means. Often, fear is about false evidence appearing real. Suppose once, when you were younger, you burned your hand on a hot radiator. It didn't feel good, so the body protects you from experiencing that feeling again and creates an association of radiators = caution. It doesn't matter whether any radiators you encounter subsequently are hot, warm, or cold; the body will approach them all as though they're red hot and have the power to hurt you again, and will react in a cautious way.

The same thing can happen with our emotions. If, as a child, you spoke your mind and someone mocked you as a result, or if you said something and were shut down, you may learn it's not okay to show your emotions as you make it uncomfortable for others or are too much. You develop a belief about yourself and how you show up and hold yourself back because you don't want to feel the caution emotion 'shame.' Shame isn't a nice feeling to experience; therefore, you avoid speaking your mind or being 'too much,' so you don't experience it, therefore shutting your emotions away.

This is why it's so important to address your upbringing and to understand (not blame) the way you've experienced the world and the beliefs you've developed about yourself, others, and the world. Reflecting on what you leave unspoken will help you see how you hold yourself back to please others. When you delve into this, you'll become more conscious of how you show up day to day and how sensitive you are to the world around you. Another important factor to acknowledge here is how we learn to regulate shame. In the past, we learned to hide it, but we can't ignore it.

CASE STUDY

Laura's been with her partner for seven years and they have a child together. Recently, she's started to get annoyed with her partner and often snaps at him. However, as soon as she lets her annoyance show, she then reverts and apologizes, blaming it on tiredness. She's avoiding the truth, which is that she's worried about upsetting her partner because she thinks he might leave if he gets fed up, as this is something she's experienced in the past.

Therefore, Laura bites her tongue, taking back her angry words, even if she's genuinely upset. She's frightened of speaking her mind and expressing her needs, because of what she thinks might happen. However, if Laura can reframe and learn that expressing how she truly feels doesn't mean her partner will leave her, she'll realize that she's worthy enough to speak her truth.

The CHILD whose emotional needs weren't met
= the ADULT who worries about upsetting
others because she fears being abandoned.

In some ways, this tool is a combination of Tools 1 and 2, in that you need to sit with yourself and consider your truest self. Consider the words you leave unspoken and why, using the questions for self-reflection below. Reflect on past experiences when you didn't speak up and consider the reasons why. If you were worried about hurting someone's feelings, ask yourself if it was really about the other person or rather your own guilt around not wanting to upset someone.

Be kind to yourself. This isn't easy. Let all the unspoken words bubble to the surface and then write them down or say them to yourself. Reflect on what they mean to you, where they come from, and why you might be letting fear hold them back.

Questions for Self-Reflection

- *What would you like to say to the world? Or to someone in particular?*

- *What are you holding back about yourself? Why are you holding back?*

- *What is it that frightens you?*

Tool 5: Don't Fight Rejection

Let's face it, nobody likes rejection. It's such an overpowering emotion. I remember how I tried to avoid it while growing up because it made me feel there was something deeply wrong with me. When you have HFA, rejection can lead to not feeling good enough, but this is something we need to change. Just because someone may not agree with us, it doesn't mean that we're not good enough.

Masking your true self as a result of fear and being who you think others need you to be just so you can avoid rejection isn't sustainable in the long run. You end up losing yourself in the process, simply because you don't want to experience rejection! We need to redefine vulnerability, learn to see it differently, and manage how we navigate our sensitivity in everyday life; this is something we'll look at in more depth in the next step.

I see rejection as an inner battle. You believe that you're not good enough and feel that others will see you the same way, so you avoid putting yourself in situations where you might be rejected. However, the only person you're really avoiding is yourself, and what you truly want. It's mind-boggling when we think of it like that!

At the beginning of this step, I shared a snippet of conversation between me and a client. While the client initially thought they were concerned about an upcoming presentation, it turned out that what really worried them was a fear of rejection by their peers. Helping them to see this allowed them to reframe their feelings around the presentation, and approach it with more confidence without fear holding them back.

CASE STUDY

Simran's trying to find a job. He's applied for roles in eight different companies but none of them have come back to him yet. Some of his friends who are also job-hunting have already had interviews and are awaiting their outcome. Simran feels like a failure and wonders what's wrong with him, and why he hasn't heard back from any of the companies to which he's applied.

He feels it's because they don't like him, and he feels rejected. However, the truth is that there are many reasons why Simran might not have heard about his job applications, but his limited view of himself has taken him straight to a place where it's his fault because he believes he's not enough.

> **The CHILD who was always criticized = the ADULT who compares himself to others and doesn't feel good enough.**

There's a famous quote by the Roman emperor and philosopher Marcus Aurelius: 'What stands in the way becomes the way.' What he meant by this is that we have the capacity to adapt to obstacles placed in our way, forging a new path. We get to *choose* how we respond. And rejection is one such obstacle. If we break it down, we have rejection = redirection. When we fear rejection, we hold ourselves back. We can't go forward, we can't be who we truly are, and we can't get past the obstacle. All we can do is walk in circles.

So, ask yourself this: *What is the worst thing that can happen if I get rejected?* It's not going to be a nice feeling, because rejection never is, but you can then choose to take that rejection and use it to move you forward, onto a different path. You can keep going. Just because there's an obstacle on this path, it doesn't mean we have to stop walking. We simply get to choose another way.

Questions for Self-Reflection

- *Reflect on a situation where you felt dismissed. Can you reframe it in a different way, so it's not about you?*

- *Is there something you're avoiding doing simply because of fear of rejection?*

- *If yes, can you approach it in a different way? Or is there another path you can take?*

Tool 6: Uncover Triggers by Exploring Your Past

When we cut ourselves off from our early anger at our caregivers for not being able to give us what we need, we also alienate or disconnect from the energy and power inside us. We replace them with behaviors designed to keep us safe, although all they actually do is hold us back. We feel shame and fear rather than expressing our true self. Our past experiences trigger behavior in the present.

Going back to our childhood and learning to understand our patterns via our everyday 'triggers' can unearth buried anger. However, anger is a secondary emotion and beneath it you'll find hurt, sadness, and pain, thus connecting with the energy we've been suppressing and allowing us to go deeper into the emotions we've buried so deep. This is a vitally important part of the healing process, as research has shown that these unreleased emotions can manifest in the body as physical illness.

Once we process the anger and pain, this connection frees the suppressed energy, reintegrating it back into our psyche. We feel more whole, alive, connected, and grounded. We can dig deeper still, reclaiming unexpressed *positive* traits that we've also hidden away and have been unable to access. By going back into the past and *unlearning* what we know, we're provided with an opportunity to rediscover parts of the self we've previously denied.

Suppose someone cheated on you or broke up with you in the past. When you go into another relationship you carry a fear of commitment, beneath which is the hurt and pain from the last relationship, especially if it was hard to 'get over.' This can trigger self-sabotaging behavior and stop you from forming meaningful relationships. Just like being burned by the hot radiator, you felt hurt and pain in the past, so now you avoid new commitments (just as you do radiators) because you don't want to feel that way again.

> **The CHILD who was heartbroken
> = the ADULT who's afraid of commitment.**

If you feel that your friends leave you out of things, or if you've been betrayed by a friend in the past, this brings up the same feeling of not being good enough, triggering behavior such as distancing yourself from people to keep yourself safe (or what you think is safe).

You've already done some digging into your past by completing the previous steps in this book. Perhaps you've discovered events that shaped you, or recognized self-sabotaging patterns of behavior that are holding you back. This is the work that needs to continue.

IDENTIFY YOUR TRIGGERS

Look back at a past relationship, whether platonic, business, or romantic, and ask yourself: *Why did I do the things I did? Why did I choose to act in that way?* Sit for a moment with the answers and see whether you can identify what triggered your actions and reactions. Don't beat yourself up, simply be with this new understanding. Write down your answers if you need to.

The more we dig, the more we learn about ourselves, and the more we learn, the more understanding we have of why we act/feel the way we do. Increased self-awareness allows us to make positive choices for ourselves, manage our guilt and shame, and release the fear that's been holding us back.

Questions for Self-Reflection

- *Do you notice any patterns in the way you relate to others?*

- *Are you holding on to something from your past that you need to let go of?*

- *What have you given up on due to fear?*

Tool 7: Unlearn Old Rules

As I explained earlier in the book, we develop beliefs about what kind of a person we are, what to expect in life, and how to relate to others based on our childhood experiences. These become the 'rules' by which we live our lives. For example, if growing up we went through some sort of unhappiness, pain, or difficulty, it can create an emotional scar, leaving us with the opinion that we're not worthy of love. This can mean that unconsciously, we try not to take up space when we're around other people because of the rule we live by. We believe that we're 'unlovable,' and each interaction we have is viewed through this lens.

Just as understanding our fear helps us to overcome it, understanding our behavior patterns and the rules we've created allows us to break them. We cycle through these past traumas, creating patterns that are supposed to help us feel safe yet doom us to relive our old feelings of sadness, worthlessness, and anger.

It's not until we bring these patterns and rules into the light that we can change them so that they no longer bind us. Knowing the root cause of our behavior and how it influences us brings us into a space of intuitive insight where we can look more objectively at our patterns and rules and better understand how they were formed. It's the first step in sorting through the rules we live by and gaining our freedom.

CASE STUDY

Tamara is having dinner with a friend who tells her how busy her week has been, and how she can't wait to get home and put on her pjs. The waitress comes to take the dinner plates and asks if they want dessert. Tamara doesn't want to take up any more of her friend's time because of what she said about being tired and wanting to go home, so she says no to dessert. This is despite the fact that she's been waiting all day to enjoy a dessert at her favorite restaurant, and she won't be able to go back there for a few months.

Why does Tamara deny herself what she really wants? Because she doesn't want to come across as taking up space and time and prefers to let her friend make the decision. Tamara is confined by the rule of wanting to be liked and not wanting to upset her friend. She could have opened up the conversation by saying, 'I know you mentioned you wanted to go to bed, but how do you feel about dessert, because it's been on my mind all day?' But instead, she chose to deny herself.

> **The CHILD who received conditional love
> = the ADULT who worries that if she
> takes up space, she'll be rejected.**

In Step 1 we looked at the various ways in which HFA manifests as different types of behavior. In Step 2 we dug deeper, into our early lives. So, by now, you should hopefully have some understanding of your behavior patterns and where they come from. If you're not yet at that point, revisit those steps and take the time you need to get to the root cause.

Once you've identified your patterns, it's time to make a conscious effort to break free of them. This will take time. You might fail a few times. You might even need external help. But the key thing is to keep going, to keep working on that understanding. Using a journal to record your efforts might be helpful, as it will be a record not just of your setbacks but also your successes and how far you've come.

Questions for Self-Reflection

Imagine you're living with a box around you.

- *What are the rules of this box?*

- *How do you show up day to day?*

- *How do you show up in front of people? How do you show up with yourself?*

- *What are your three rules of life and how do you think these rules limit you or expand you?*

Tool 8: Implement Boundaries

Implementing boundaries means, essentially, making decisions about what we feel we can and cannot deal with in our lives. It's important to note that boundaries can only be implemented on ourselves – they are our own choice and can't be used to try and control the behaviors of others. Our response *is* the boundary.

It's also important to note that we implement boundaries based on our self-worth. If we have low self-worth (as many with HFA do) or feel we need to earn self-worth from others, our boundaries will define this. We might tolerate things we wouldn't normally put up with, simply to feel good enough. However, the more we learn self-respect and develop a better relationship with ourselves, the more our boundaries will change and the stronger they'll become.

As we unlearn unhealthy forms of attachment within our relationships, we also learn how to create new boundaries. We no longer get lost in wanting to be enough, or showing up as what we think the other person wants us to be. We no longer accept crumbs; instead, we want our own slice of cake.

For example, in a romantic relationship you might continually go along with what your partner wants, regardless of your own wishes, simply because you don't wish to upset them or be rejected; or you may believe your own needs aren't worthy of being met.

> The CHILD who grew up feeling they were 'too much'
> = the ADULT who fears speaking out because they worry
> about upsetting their partner and the partner leaving.

But when you break free from this pattern, you show up differently. You no longer worry about whether you're good enough or about rejection; instead, you go with what feels right and how you can communicate, leading to healthier relationship-building going forward. This is true of all kinds of relationships, not just romantic ones.

Questions for Self-Reflection

Consider an important relationship in your life, whether it's platonic, romantic, or professional. Really look at it objectively. Then ask yourself the questions below. Explore not only the behavior of the other person but also your own. Be honest. I've recommended writing things down before, and I do think it can bring clarity; however, simply sitting with yourself and asking these questions will also open you to the truth of the matter.

- *Do you feel as though your needs have equal weight within the relationship?*

- *Are you able to express to the other person how you truly feel?*

- *What boundaries do you have in place? What boundaries would you like to change or implement?*

- *What worries you most about the relationship?*

- *What patterns are you bringing from previous relationships?*

- *Is there anything you'd like to change about the relationship?*

Tool 9: Own Your Worth

Don't dim your light to try and feel 'enough' for those around you. You can't expect everyone to get you or to connect with you. Owning this changes how you show up. You don't need to personalize how others behave toward/around you.

This is your opportunity to find the power within yourself to direct your life. To feel grounded from within. Imagine if you were to try to push down a tree (not that you would, but bear with me), but found you couldn't because the roots were so deep in the soil – you too can be like this! Use this and the other tools to discover your inner strength and a sense of independence which will help you to gain a new sense of direction or purpose.

As I've mentioned, it can be difficult to let go of familiar structures and ways of being, even if they no longer work for us. But these structures are keeping you in the shadows. It's time to emerge into the fullness of your own light and own who you truly are. You have so much more to offer, so don't hold back any longer.

CASE STUDY

Every time Rohit goes out with his friends he offers to drive. Sometimes he asks his friends to drive instead, but they always come back and ask him to do it, so he agrees as he doesn't want to upset them.

Rohit always feels tired after a long day of driving his friends around. Also, his friends talk about topics that he doesn't find interesting, but he tries to stay involved in the conversation as he doesn't want to feel left out or be excluded. However, by not speaking out about how he truly feels about always being the driver, or not talking about things that he enjoys, Rohit is dimming his light, simply because he's worried about upsetting his friends. He's not owning his worth.

The CHILD who received conditional love = the ADULT who dims his light to fit in and feel good enough.

I'm telling you that you *are* enough. That you have all that you need inside you. That the past no longer needs to limit you. Take a moment and sit with yourself. Look into a mirror, or simply close your eyes, and tell yourself, 'I'm enough. I'm capable. I'm worthy. I choose to let my light shine.' Remind yourself of all that you've achieved. You don't need to hide any more.

Questions for Self-Reflection

- *Where do you notice that you hold yourself back?*

- *Where do you notice that you dim your light? Is there anyone in particular you do this around? And if so, what do you think it is about this person that drives this behavior?*

- *What worries you about what others might think about you?*

- *What's the worst thing someone could say about you, and why is this important to you?*

Tool 10: Be Honest with Yourself

Only when we begin to be honest with ourselves can we start to change. And I mean truly, deeply honest. This isn't about anyone else; it's only about you. Only you can do this for yourself. As I've explained, it will probably be a difficult process at times, as this type of self-analysis can bring old issues to the surface – deep issues that you've tried to keep buried. However, it's only by facing these issues, by no longer hiding them away, that you can truly break free. But to get there requires honesty on your part, and no more running away.

The thing with having HFA is that we're already coming from a place of low self-esteem and wanting to please others. We've almost forgotten how it feels to be honest with ourselves. But if we go back to that butterfly waiting in its cocoon to emerge, it becomes apparent how necessary this period of deep and honest introspection is in terms of emerging as our best selves. It's our opportunity to come to terms with the wounds of the past and the patterns of the present. To admit, as difficult as it might be, that we're not perfect. No one is. But admitting it is a step toward once more feeling that sense of power and faith in ourselves that was quashed by our early experiences.

CASE STUDY

Sam, who for years went along with what others wanted and never made choices for herself, must now decide where she wants to go, what she wants to do, and what she enjoys. She feels overwhelmed by these choices, as she doesn't know what she wants. But this is okay. Think of it as like dating someone and getting to know them. You can't be expected to know everything right off the bat, and it's the same as you get to know this new version of you. Part of the journey of life involves being patient and learning along the way. We don't need to have it all figured out.

> **The CHILD who never felt she could ask for what she wanted = the ADULT who's overwhelmed by and cannot advocate for her needs.**

Each tool in this step is an exercise in being honest with yourself. So, if you've gone through Tools 1 to 9, you've dug pretty deep. The key now is to keep going with it. Be honest in your interactions, in how you present to the world, in how you speak to yourself. Let go of the lies you used to tell yourself in order to feel safe; things like, *I'm not good enough. My feelings don't matter. It will be better if I don't do that.* All they do is hold you back.

SELF-REFLECTION MOOD BOARD

It's time to get creative and make a mood board. Write your name in the center of a piece of card or paper, and then around it add more words and pictures that you feel represent who you are (you can cut pictures out of magazines or add them digitally if you're doing this online).

Now imagine that you're going to present this mood board to someone, and it's vitally important that you show them how you see yourself. It might feel daunting at first, especially if you've never really spoken about yourself before. But guess what? It's time to feel the fear and show up anyway – as yourself.

And there you have it. A tool kit to help you as you take your first steps toward learning to let go, choose honesty, establish healthy boundaries, and feel good enough.

STEP 3 SUMMARY

Take a moment to congratulate yourself for getting to the end of Step 3. If you've been working your way through the self-reflection questions, you'll have faced quite a bit of your shadow side, something that isn't easy to do. However, this step is such an important one in your process toward integrating the two sides of yourself and living a life free of fear, limiting rules, and self-doubt. It's time to let the old structures that bound you fall away, in order to make space for the new.

Now the learning continues. In Step 4, we're going to continue the process of working with this new version of you. If, like many of my clients, you're not quite sure who that is yet, that's okay. Take your time. Be in the chrysalis until it's time to emerge. We're still very much on the journey. Are you ready to emerge into the light?

STEP 4

Embrace Your Sensitivity and Reclaim Self-Trust

In Steps 1 to 3 we talked a lot about how our childhood shapes us, and the fact that people with HFA tend to be highly sensitive people. In Step 4, I'd like to expand a little more on what I mean by 'highly sensitive.'

A highly sensitive person is likely to feel things more deeply, whether those things are positive or negative. While the highs can be joyous, the lows can present challenges which affect our stress levels, relationships, and ability to cope. With HFA, our highly sensitive side is the one we've learned to hide away because we feel it's too much, when in fact it's the part of us that carries the wisdom of sensitivity. It's this wisdom that helps us to navigate deeper, more meaningful relationships.

For me, everything changed when I understood this. I was able to finally get out of living in my head, telling myself stories to fill the gaps. I stopped running away from my sensitivity and instead embraced the things I was actually feeling. This is why the next step in the process is to embrace your sensitivity.

Giving Space to Sensitivity

Let's break down what sensitivity means. At its core, it's a connection via the senses with the outside world, and something that every human being experiences. If we're more, or highly, sensitive, it may be because we're more attuned to other people and can notice subtle things such as changes in tone of voice or body language.

When we don't understand our sensitivity, though, what often happens is that we put on our blue-tinted glasses and equate a change in someone with the belief that we've done something wrong. **A change in someone = I've done something wrong.** This is the equation that we need to alter.

In Step 2, I spoke about how I felt that my family couldn't hold a safe space for me, and that I chose to make myself smaller as a result; while in Step 3 we went deeper into our childhood experiences, peeling back the layers to expose our sensitive cores and the fears we live by in order to try and protect ourselves. Making sense of this and gaining understanding gives us the tools we need to face our challenges with strength. In the vulnerability of sensitivity lies the strength to rise above shame, transforming whispers of doubt into a symphony of empowerment.

In Step 4, we're going to learn how to hold our sensitivity and give it space to be. To not lock it away any longer but bring it, blinking, from the shadows to the light. It might hurt a little, because things are all rather raw and new, but the discomfort will be temporary. You deserve this, especially after the years of anxiety, guilt, and shame you're now learning to release.

Instead of retreating into uncertainty and fear, you'll learn to trust yourself. You'll listen to what your sensitivity is trying to tell you rather than listening to stories created by your fear. This is your time to stand in the light, without your constant fear dimming you. Fear is no longer in the driving seat. *You* are. Fear remains as a passenger, to whom you can choose to listen, but you're the driver.

> *Embrace your sensitivity with an open heart,*
> *for it's the key to unlocking the treasures*
> *of empathy and deep connection.*

Rise above shame and you'll discover the strength to shine, unapologetically, as the vibrant soul you were always meant to be. The number one rule here is this: do not take the changes that you see in others personally. Whatever's going on for someone else is their journey and path. And how you react belongs to you. Cut the emotional cord. Let people be. The work here is to observe and make space – space where it's possible to receive feedback and look at it critically rather than taking it to heart. Where feedback can offer you something, and where you can also recognize when it's not about you.

Making space requires us to be gentle with ourselves, accept that we're human, and create the capacity to take ownership and accountability for ourselves. It also requires us to pick ourselves back up and not have our worth defined by the stories we create to fill the gap.

There's Nothing Wrong with You

I'll say it louder for the people in the back: **THERE'S NOTHING WRONG WITH YOU. YOU ARE ENOUGH!** I've mentioned several times that clients who present with HFA often feel that something's wrong but they're not sure what. It's so sad to live in this way – where every move or interaction you have with someone comes with a deep sense of worry that you might be doing it wrong, or a fear of what they might think of you. How can you 'just be' when you have this cord of worry that's always connected to others? People with HFA struggle to believe in themselves.

For highly sensitive individuals, such as those of us with HFA, our first assumption when someone doesn't give us what we need is that it's because something's wrong with us, or we've *done* something wrong. We go straight into feeling that we're lacking in some way, which is a reflection of how we feel about ourselves.

It's as though the core belief we carry shines through and is projected into the external world. This then develops into the HFA behaviors I've already described – tying ourselves in knots to try and get our needs met, when in fact, we can't control other people's responses to our need.

What we must do is *reframe* this way of thinking and untie the knots. Rather than our immediate reaction being, 'What's wrong with me?' instead, we need to consciously change our thoughts by understanding what's *actually* going on in the situation and being curious about what we might be reacting to.

This isn't something that will happen overnight; it takes time, and there will be moments when you find yourself falling back into the old space of 'What's wrong with me?' Don't be too hard on yourself when this happens; it's all part of the process, and you now have the self-awareness and the tools to climb back out and think differently.

Navigating Our Sensitivity

While I was growing up, I learned that I needed to switch off from my sensitivity because I didn't know how to listen to it. I tried to shut it away, which ended up becoming a battle of me vs. my sensitivity. I felt I was weak for feeling and showing my emotions, so I pretended they didn't exist, while at the same time feeling so disconnected within.

For example, when I was upset, I learned to hide it because I felt I'd be rejected or judged, as being upset was not the norm in my family. I *created* this rule as a result of these feelings because I feared being vulnerable. I found a temporary way to cope and, when I look back at that version of me who put up these walls, I offer her compassion. I get what she did with the limited tools and understanding she had – she found a way to survive. All I wanted was to be loved and cared for. But I also needed people to accept me in order to feel good enough. This meant I was constantly watching people for their reactions to me, which then became the patterns that continued into adulthood.

Let me give you an example of my heightened sensitivity. Once, I was talking to a friend about what she'd been up to, both of us engaged in the conversation. But when the discussion turned to what I'd been doing, she took out her phone, saying she just needed to check something. I interpreted this as 'she's not interested in what I'm saying,' so I stopped talking about myself and brought the conversation back to her.

This interaction confirmed my core belief that 'I'm not important enough to take up space' or 'people don't care about me,' fueling my perception that I wasn't enough. Can you see how I ended up in a space where I believed I had to adjust my behavior because my friend became 'unavailable' when she took out her phone? The point is that there are so many ways to navigate relationships instead of shutting down or dimming our light.

My journey toward change began when, instead of reacting and jumping to conclusions in my head, I listened to what I was experiencing. I became curious about my feelings and thoughts. I was open to understanding myself instead of shaming myself. And I need to share with you how important it is to be patient with yourself. I was frustrated by the fact that I had all this new understanding but still fell into what I call the Rabbit Hole of Doom at times (even if doing so unlocked another layer of learning and compassion).

Today, instead of assuming that something's wrong with me, I sit with my experience and ask myself what makes me feel that something's wrong. Recalling the example with my friend, I'd now say something like, 'I really want to continue talking about me, but

I notice you've taken out your phone, which has distracted me. I can see it's distracted you, too. Do you need some time to catch up and we can then continue our conversation?'

Of course, what someone else might say in a similar scenario depends on the relationship they hold with that friend and other experiences they've had. But the point is that we're in charge, and we can use the nudge from our sensitivity to help guide the way we navigate it. We can make a choice to step away from our default response and, most of the time, we'll find a way to navigate and develop the deeper connections we yearn for.

Climb Out of the Rabbit Hole of Doom

Here's another example of how we can try to better navigate the heightened sensitivity of HFA. Imagine you're talking to a friend, but they don't seem to be engaging with you in the way they usually do.

- **Sensitivity default**: Your friend doesn't like you – you're talking too much and you're losing them. You've shared too much, and they think you're stupid.

- **Reality**: Your friend is hungover from a big night out and, as much as they love you, they don't have as much energy as usual for a chat.

- **Answer**: Instead of pivoting to the sensitivity default, listen to what your sensitivity is telling you. Ask your friend if they're okay instead of being so hard on yourself.

In the depths of darkness, we find the strength to climb out of the Rabbit Hole of Doom, emerging into the light of hope and resilience. Of course, navigating our sensitivity is easier said than done and, just like anything, it will take practice for us to become comfortable with integrating it into our lives.

There will be times when you 'fall down' the Rabbit Hole of Doom, and I want you to be mindful of how you treat yourself and what you say to yourself when you do, as there's another layer of growth here. Remember that no one's perfect – you're human and have lived for years with high expectations of yourself, so naturally, when things don't go exactly to plan, you can fall back into thinking there's something wrong with you. But you have the choice of either going down the rabbit hole or taking another path.

Each time this happens, you might fall a little less down the rabbit hole before you realize what's going on. This is you growing.

Growth doesn't always come from actions; it can also come from your awareness of the situation and your understanding of what's actually going on for you.

There will still be times when you misread a situation or default to your old reactions, heading down the rabbit hole, and that's all part of the process. In the dance of life's challenges, we can choose to step back from the edge of the rabbit hole, embrace awareness to break free from its grip, and create a different path toward resilience and growth. In the tangled web of despair, let courage be your guide as you break free, discovering the radiant light that awaits beyond.

Let's look at another example. Suppose one day you come home from work and your partner doesn't give you a hug. Instantly, your brain goes into overdrive, thinking, *Did I do something wrong? He's been very quiet lately. Maybe he doesn't love me anymore.*

This is the first step down the Rabbit Hole of Doom and, the deeper we go, the more stories we find to tell ourselves. *I must have annoyed him when I spoke about my work. If he leaves me, I'll have to move back to my parents' house. I knew I wasn't good enough – I should have done more XYZ.*

As a result of these thoughts, we can end up shutting down or distancing ourselves from our partner as a form of protection. But can you see that we've *created* these non-existent scenarios? Our sensitivity has noticed that our partner isn't okay, but instead of asking them, 'Hey, you didn't give me a hug today. Is everything all right?' we've chosen to fall back into old patterns, getting caught up in our imagination and making the situation worse.

However, even if you're partway down the rabbit hole, you can still pull yourself out. All it takes is being conscious enough to say to yourself, *Hang on a moment. This might not be about me.* Instead of using your sensitivity to take you on a ride, realize that what it's actually doing is helping you to understand that something isn't right, and then choose to communicate that.

HFA and Healthy Boundaries

Just as fences keep things safe, setting firm personal boundaries will protect you, shutting out energies that don't serve you.

It's important, however, to remember that boundaries aren't something you can impose on others. Boundaries are your own responses to behavior around you, as you decide what you will and won't tolerate within your life. It's time to learn to put yourself first without feeling selfish. Only you can decide what your boundaries are, and these can be changed as you continue to evolve. Boundaries are like a muscle – the more you use them, the stronger they become.

In the past, I'd have tried to hold on to something that wasn't working for me out of fear. But now I know it's essential to let go and move on when necessary. Of course, I still get the little niggle of 'what if' in the back of my mind, but it doesn't drive me to hold on tighter. If I notice myself wanting to do so, I sit with this reflection to make sense of it. My boundaries have become stronger because I'm taking time to understand my needs before responding to them.

Amid the ebb and flow of life, setting boundaries helps us to forge a solid foundation of self-care and meaningful connections.

In Step 1, we looked at seven different types of what I call the two-sided behavior of HFA. For each one I shared a client case study, 'Sara.' We can also use these and the case study to explore how to set healthy boundaries – let's see how, once we've recognized a certain pattern of behavior, we can then set boundaries which will help us to change it.

HFA Behavior Type 1

The over-responsible one vs. the one who can manage everything

My client Sara was struggling with her workload; however, analysis revealed that much of it was things she had to do for other people, which she'd taken on as she felt guilty about saying 'no.' It even involved taking on a co-worker's entire workload while they were on sick leave, which led to Sara feeling completely exhausted. She did this because she wanted to be seen as someone who could 'do it all,' and she also wanted to make others feel good.

The Boundary

This one involves the word 'no.' It's strange that such a small word can be so difficult for many of to use. We worry about how others might feel, without stopping to consider how *we* feel. We often say 'yes' because we don't want to be judged as inadequate or feel that we're letting someone down. We agree to do things when we shouldn't, when our plates are already overloaded, simply because we don't want to be seen as 'less than' in any way.

There's an example of this I often cite. You don't leave the front door of your house open so that anyone can come in, so why do you allow others to encroach on your time and space in the real world? Saying 'no' is one of the strongest things you can do. It sets a firm boundary and allows you to express how you truly feel about a situation. All in a one-syllable word. Pretty powerful, eh?

SETTING THE BOUNDARY

Try using the word 'no' in one of your everyday interactions. It's important to use it only when you're being asked to do something that's outside your remit or isn't your responsibility. While it might feel strange at first, you'll get better at it with practice. At first, the guilt may be overwhelming, but just sit with your feelings and let them flow. You can do this.

HFA Behavior Type 2

The controller vs. the high achiever

Sara was seen as a leader and a high achiever in her workplace. In reality, though, she overthought everything, leading to anxiety and an inability to maintain a healthy work-life balance. She was working almost constantly just to keep up with this external expectation and spent time thinking about all the scenarios that could possibly happen – to the point where her quality of life was affected.

The Boundary

The importance of setting a work-life boundary is something we hear a lot about, yet it's not always clear how to do this, especially in our 24-hour, on-demand digital world. Work-life boundaries can include the following: setting a time each day after which you don't check work emails or respond to calls (letting clients/co-workers know via automatic replies and answering messages); keeping to working hours as closely as possible; and setting specific time aside each week for leisure activities.

SETTING THE BOUNDARY

If you're prone to overthinking, make an appointment with yourself (and yes, I mean schedule it in your diary) and set a time to think about the issue at hand. Then, each time it pops into your head, tell yourself, *I'll think about that at (appointment time)*. Repeat as necessary. Then, when the appointment time arrives, spend 10 minutes (or a duration of your choice) on the issue and afterward, let it go.

HFA Behavior Type 3

The perfectionist vs. the hard worker

Sara had extremely high expectations of herself and when she didn't reach them, would mentally castigate herself. She told me when she first came to therapy that she wanted 'to be fixed' because she wasn't successful.

Perfectionism is part of HFA because it's about how we want to show up for others – essentially, it's people-pleasing. As we discussed in Step 2, this is one of the behaviors we learn when we're young to protect ourselves. But it's just not possible to spend your life chasing people's reactions to you in order to feel good enough. You end up living for others and your perception of what they think, and in the process become further disconnected from yourself.

The Boundary

This boundary is one that you need to set with yourself and be conscious about enforcing. Perfectionists are very hard on themselves; they have high expectations and don't want to be seen as a failure and, as a result, feel a need to control every aspect of their life. However, this simply isn't realistic, and it doesn't support ongoing mental health. So, the boundary you need to set is one of kindness to yourself.

Accept that you'll fail sometimes, that things will happen that are beyond your control. And when they do, be kind to yourself. Listen to how you speak to yourself when things fall outside your control, as this is where your learning will take place.

So far, you've done the best you can with the tools you have. Now you have new tools that you may not know how to use as easily as the old ones, but I promise they will help you. They will also help you to celebrate what you've achieved rather than obsessing over what you haven't. Look at what you have in the glass already, rather than focusing on how you're going to fill it.

SETTING THE BOUNDARY

When you have HFA, chances are there's something right now that you're not happy about, and which you're overthinking. Perhaps you didn't achieve that promotion you wanted, or you let someone down despite your best efforts, or you don't have time to get all your jobs done because you've set such a high expectation for yourself.

Perhaps your appearance isn't how you want it to be. Or you're comparing yourself to others who seem to have their lives in order and criticizing yourself for not being like them.

STOP! Instead of beating yourself up about it, try this instead. Put your hand on your heart, feel it beating, and use your compassionate side to tell yourself that it's okay. And *mean* it. Remind yourself of your life experiences and all the things you've been through to get where you are now.

You didn't get the promotion, but you were good enough to be considered for it. Your hair might not look like that of some of the people on Instagram, but you have a beautiful smile. Remember, life throws us curveballs all the time; what's important is how we react when they come to us. It's like a running tap; if we try to grab hold of the water, it leaves us frustrated because we just can't do it. We can't always hold on to the things we want in life, either. Let them go.

HFA Behavior Type 4

The excessive worrier vs. the unflappable one

While Sara appeared to be successful and in control on the surface, she told me that she felt her brain was 'always on,' constantly worrying about what others thought of her, or of what might happen in any given situation. This constant worry stems, like so much of HFA, from fear, and a barrage of 'what if?' questions constantly posed by the anxious mind. This anxiety can then snowball, leaving us feeling exhausted and overwhelmed, and unable to manage our thoughts.

The Boundary

It can be difficult to get out of this pattern of intrusive thoughts and sometimes it takes external help to get there. However, while you can't control what your mind throws at you, you can control how much attention you give to your thoughts. As we grow in consciousness and understanding of our behavior patterns, it becomes easier to notice when our thoughts are trying to undermine us.

Set a boundary that you'll give your thoughts less attention. It might seem difficult and overwhelming at first but, with practice, it will become easier. Just as you taught yourself to think in a certain way, so you can do the same again.

SETTING THE BOUNDARY

This exercise is similar to the one for HFA Behavior Type 1, in that in consists of saying 'no.' However, this time, the word is in your mind rather than the physical world. Practice saying 'no' and meaning it. Picture yourself holding up your hand, or closing a door, or any other image that works for you. Do it until it feels natural for you. Then, the next time you start to spiral into worrying thoughts, tell your mind 'no,' just as you've practiced, and see what happens.

In my work, I often draw on an aspect of the cartoon *Inside Out* as a way to set this boundary (if you haven't watched it, please take some time to do so, as it has some powerful scenes). The main character in the film experiences different emotions, each of which also appears as a character. One of the 'emotion' characters is Fear, who's always scanning for the worst-case scenario.

You can try creating a character for your fear. Then, when it comes to the surface, you can compassionately remind it that everything's okay. This is part of self-soothing and self-regulating our emotions. Externalizing our fear helps because rather than it being enmeshed in our mind, it can be broken down and more easily processed and managed. You can even try writing it down; create two columns, one for your fear and the other for your compassion, and then have a conversation with self from these two parts of you.

HFA Behavior Type 5

The fearful one vs. the successful one

Sara blamed herself when things went wrong, keeping a mental file of all her perceived failures, which she'd take out and look at, like flawed gemstones. She'd get upset and angry with herself and spent time thinking of all the things she could have done differently to change a situation, even though it was long past.

Imagine keeping a mental file like this, where you store all those things you think make you not good enough, and when you have time to think, you go through the drawers. What a way to live! It's a form of psychological torture that you wouldn't dream of inflicting on anyone else, yet you allow it for yourself. And, if you allow this, how do you allow others to treat you?

As I explained in Step 1, fear of failure is a behavior we learn in order to protect ourselves. It can be embarrassing to fail, and it can make us feel angry, upset, or frustrated with ourselves. However, failure is part of life. It's how we learn. If we focus so much on failure and how it makes others see us, it can lead to us no longer wanting to try anything new – in case we fail again. But by doing this we're letting our fear hold us back. This is no way to live life, nervously stepping forward while trying to avoid the *possibility* of failure, behaving cautiously 'just in case.' We need to learn to trust that, whatever happens, we'll be able to process and get through it in one piece.

The Boundary

As we've discussed, choosing not to try anything new, procrastinating about doing tasks, or chasing 'success' at all costs are boundaries set by our fear. We fear the feeling of failure because it reinforces our core belief that we're not good enough. So, we do all that we can to avoid it. But, instead of staying inside this fear boundary, what we need to do is step outside it.

The next time your mind tells you that you shouldn't try something because you might fail and that doing so would be awful, or tells you to chase something you want to achieve at all costs, take a moment to consciously STOP, PAUSE, and REFLECT. Recognize that these thoughts come from within the fear boundary and, as I recommended in the previous exercise, externalize the fear to help you manage it.

Remember, you're the one in the driver's seat; fear is just a passenger, and it doesn't get to decide where you go. Step outside and look at things from a compassionate perspective; if this was a friend's choice to make, how would you advise them? This is the process of learning to trust yourself and proceed with an open heart rather than one closed by fear.

SETTING THE BOUNDARY

Is there something you've always wanted to try but fear is holding you back? Or is there something you're desperate to achieve yet have failed to do so? In the case of the former, try it. And if you do fail, take a moment to feel the failure, experience the emotions, and notice what you say to yourself as a result. Are you being critical, or putting yourself down? Again, imagine this is a friend who has come to you – how would you respond to them? With compassion, right?

Maybe it's time to use the skills we use with others on ourselves. This exercise is about becoming familiar with the fear, so it no longer has the power to scare you and you don't need to run from it. It's about learning to trust yourself when failure happens, so that you can regulate through it and soothe yourself in a healthy way.

HFA Behavior Type 6

The disappointer vs. the one with healthy boundaries

Sara struggled with setting boundaries around her time and space out of fear of disappointing others, which led to anxiety. Through her sessions with me, she realized that she wanted to appear 'available' at all times – so as not to disappoint other people – while disregarding her own feelings.

Not wanting to disappoint others is a natural feeling. However, doing things that we don't want to do, or which impact our own lives in a disruptive way, simply to try and please other people, means that, inevitably, we disappoint ourselves instead. The fact is, we can't control how other people feel about us. There's nothing selfish about choosing to set healthy boundaries around what you can give others in terms of your time and energy. In fact, it's part of being true to yourself.

The Boundary

Quite a few of the boundaries in this section can be enforced simply by asking yourself *What's my intention?* whenever you agree to do something. If you find that your intention is to do what you *believe* is expected because you're worrying about what someone else might think, then you know what you need to do. Set a boundary where you say, 'No, thank you,' because it doesn't align with you. Of course, you'll then need to sit with the discomfort and guilt about disappointing others. However, with compassion and the tools in this section, you can work through it.

In an authentic life, *you* get to choose how much of your time, space, and energy you give to others. HFA can cause you to give too much of yourself away, leaving barely anything for you. This pattern is what you take into your personal and work relationships. But it's time to reclaim yourself. Time and energy are your currency – how are you going to spend it? Make sure, when you're saying yes to something, that it's done from a place of intention and self-compassion, which in itself is part of the learning process.

SETTING THE BOUNDARY

Look at your diary for the next few days, week, or month. How many of the things in it did you say 'yes' to because you wanted to (or were required to, such as work commitments)? Explore how each 'yes' makes you feel. Again, ask yourself whether if this was a friend, you'd tell them to do things differently or make suggestions for change. Are there changes that you can make?

Alternatively, journal your day and make a note of the times when you feel you're doing something because you don't want to make someone unhappy (such as stopping for a conversation when you'd rather be working or reading), instead of it being something *you* want to do. Can you set a compassionate boundary around your time and energy?

HFA Behavior Type 7

The overachiever vs. the one who has it all

Sara was celebrated in her workplace and was generally seen as someone who 'got things done.' Yet all of this came at a cost to her well-being and mental health. Years of taking on work she didn't actually have the time to do had left no space for a personal or romantic life; nor did she have time to check in with herself and make sure that her goals were of her own choosing rather than based on the expectations of others. She kept herself as busy as she could, so she didn't have to stop and sit in the space of not being good enough.

The Boundary

In life, we can sometimes feel that a role or expectation is placed on us, whether by our parents, employer, or friends. Often it has to do with achieving certain goals or living a specific type of lifestyle. If these goals are something you also truly feel in your heart and want to chase, then by all means go for it. However, making sure you have the time to check in with yourself periodically is important, as is making time to see family and friends, or to have a romantic relationship if you wish to. I call these *pause moments*, where you allow time to check in with yourself, just as you do with other people.

HFA can lead us to forget about our own needs – especially when an expectation is placed on us, as we'll then do all we can to achieve the goals, even at the expense of our personal lives. The problem is, as I've said before, when achievement is associated with short bursts of feeling good enough, it's just a temporary fix, as our real belief is that we *aren't* good enough at all.

When you're in the space of 'achieving' it can be uncomfortable to stop because when you do, you feel confused about who you are or what you want, as you've never given yourself the space to learn about your likes and dislikes. It's easier to stay on the hamster wheel and chase temporary fixes than face your real feelings. So, you feel stuck and, as a result, stay on the wheel.

SETTING THE BOUNDARY

Intentionally set yourself some pause moments in your diary. Use these to check in with yourself and ask the questions below (please note you can adjust the wording of these to fit you):

Part 1

- Do I feel that I have enough time to do things for me right now, away from work and other responsibilities? If not, why not? What can I do to change this?

- Do I feel that I'm chasing achievements to feel good enough?

- What's happened this week that I'm proud of and why?

- Do I need to give myself more of something right now?

- How do I feel my work-life balance is right now?

- How did I show up for me this week?

Once you've answered these questions, it might also be useful to sit with yourself and consider how you live your life. Set a timer, say for 10 minutes, and in that time check in with how you're feeling that day. Do so with curiosity and without judgment. See what comes to the surface, and how it makes you feel.

Part 2

Next, keep a diary – for a week or a month, whatever suits you – in which you account for how you spend your time each day. How much time is spent with friends? Sleeping? Doing something you love? Exercising? Working? A healthy life work-balance should feature time for yourself as well as for work. You may be in an industry that requires long working hours, but you should still be able to make time for you.

Now use the insights you've gained in Parts 1 and 2 to make a decision: how many hours do you wish to spend doing the things you do each week/month? And how do they compare with the actual totals? Then set your boundary and adjust your time wherever possible. Start living your life for you.

Setting boundaries can feel uncomfortable or even selfish at first, as they are decisions made to benefit your feelings. However, there's nothing wrong in choosing to set a healthy boundary – once you understand the need to do so. This is your life, and each day you spend chasing the validation of others to feel 'enough' is one less day to find that self-compassion, love, and acceptance inside yourself.

Reframing Fear Thoughts

I've mentioned the idea of reframing our thoughts, or 'cognitive reframing,' several times already, but it's one of those things that's easier said than done. It requires us to adjust our perception of a situation and see it from a different point of view, and it can only really be done effectively once we understand where our initial feelings come from.

Here's an example of cognitive reframing. Imagine a couple who are both employed, live a good life, and have a positive work-life balance. But then one of them has an operation, after which there are complications, and they need to take more time off work and become more dependent on their partner. This means the still-working partner must be at home more often, take on more of the household chores, and put up with changes in their partner's mood.

Now, the person who's taking on all the additional work feels unappreciated and no longer has a good work-life balance; and both parties are feeling irritable and are barely talking to one another. Instead of making space to hold one other, their relationship becomes filled with resentment and unspoken words. The smallest of things causes disruption because they can no longer communicate effectively.

And when we add HFA into the mix, it becomes even more complicated. If we understand that the person who had the operation grew up with a parent who, whenever they got cross, refused to speak to their child, we can see how much additional distress would be created by them now receiving the same treatment from their partner. They learned that they needed to please others to get their emotional needs met, but now they're stuck in a situation where, no matter what they do, they can't please their partner.

And perhaps the other person was constantly let down by their parent, and consequently found it difficult to trust others. They learned that they had to take care of everything themselves. Now, when they've decided to trust someone enough to form a relationship with them, they're being let down again. Even though it's not the other person's fault, their HFA causes them to withdraw. Only by gaining this understanding of each other will this couple be able to reframe their situation and break free from the harmful patterns of HFA behavior. Once again, this goes back to how our childhood experiences inform patterns of behavior through to adulthood.

Here's another example of cognitive reframing. The COVID-19 pandemic was a difficult time for us all, and the various lockdowns only added to feelings of isolation for many. The model below demonstrates how it's possible to make a cognitive adjustment to our point of view, changing our negative thoughts about lockdowns into more positive ones.

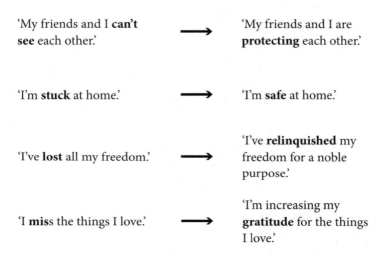

'My friends and I **can't see** each other.' ⟶ 'My friends and I are **protecting** each other.'

'I'm **stuck** at home.' ⟶ 'I'm **safe** at home.'

'I've **lost** all my freedom.' ⟶ 'I've **relinquished** my freedom for a noble purpose.'

'I **miss** the things I love.' ⟶ 'I'm increasing my **gratitude** for the things I love.'

Cognitive Reframing

Managing an Eruption of Feelings

When aspects of the self that have been held in check or ignored for a long time eventually erupt into our consciousness, they may at first do so in an awkward, imbalanced, or uncontrollable manner. For example, if your tendency in the past has been to put your own needs aside for the sake of others, you could swing too far in the opposite direction. No longer willing to take a back seat in life, you could go wild with your newfound assertiveness: it's your turn to call the shots and you react with anger or resentment if anyone gets in your way or doesn't respect you in the way you expect.

Your relationship with your worth is changing, and it will ripple out to affect others. You might demand that everyone adjusts to you rather than you adjusting to everyone else, but this can cause friction.

Imagine that others have always seen you as the color blue and treat you based on that. However, now you're showing up as yellow and acting in a whole new way. Yet the people around you don't realize at first that anything's changed, and they continue to treat you as blue. This can lead to you feeling resentful, restricted, and limited. However, it's neither your fault nor theirs. Your personal evolution needs to come with communication, not red-hot lava.

In my work, I've often seen how a disruption like this can lead to lessons in understanding ourselves and, ultimately, growth. This is not a time to inhibit or sacrifice our inner needs and desires for the sake of keeping the peace or making people happy. We need to listen to and finally respect what's happening inside us, make space for ourselves, and wake up to who we are.

You are deserving of space, deserving of love, and worthy of feeling good enough.

People may not like you changing or not behaving in your set of predictable patterns, but there's no way around it. You need to sit with this discomfort in order to regulate through it.

My research at university was about how when someone develops their self-awareness, it can impact their interpersonal relationships. I found this fascinating, as I'd noticed it in my own life – the way my friend circle changed and how I was showing up differently. I remember feeling disconnected and as if I no longer fitted in. I also see this with clients; when they start realizing their worth and connecting with their values, they start to question the relationships they have with the people around them.

Once this 'volcanic' stage eventually passes, you begin to learn how to use your new, assertive energy more wisely and skillfully. You begin to integrate this knowledge into how you live your life, learning to speak out. It's an ongoing journey, as everyone you encounter is different. Ultimately, however, you realize that control lies not in trying to manage how others respond, but in how you sway in the wind, following your own heart.

This change isn't easy, especially if we've derived our sense of worth, safety, and security from these old patterns of behavior. You might feel fear and anxiety around this disruption at first, but it's important to remember that it will lead to positive change. This is the darkness before the dawn, so to speak. You'll learn that there are other ways to develop your self-esteem, unrelated to how others think of you, as well as ways to develop new skills and abilities that you might not have normally explored.

How Self-Awareness Unveils Grief and Loss

As we develop our self-awareness, we notice the way we allow others to treat us. It can be both eye-opening and challenging to see the dynamics of our relationships more clearly. We may become frustrated with ourselves for not recognizing certain red flags earlier, but it's essential to remember that our needs and perspectives may have been different at that time.

In the process of healing and self-discovery, we start to understand that seeking validation from others may have been a significant factor in our tolerating certain behaviors. However, as we grow, we learn to meet our own needs for validation and begin to value ourselves more. This newfound self-respect may prompt us to shed the patterns and behaviors that no longer serve us.

While this journey can bring grief and sadness, it also brings excitement for the potential that lies ahead. As we let go of relationships that no longer align with our growth, we create space for new and healthier connections to emerge. Some friends may evolve alongside us, supporting our growth, while others may naturally drift away.

Feeling selfish during this process is normal, as we prioritize our well-being and growth. It's crucial to recognize, though, that taking care of ourselves and setting boundaries are acts of self-love, not selfishness. Through this journey, we learn to honor ourselves, build healthier relationships, and create a more authentic and fulfilling life.

CASE STUDY

I worked with Mya, who'd always followed everything that her mother had told her to do based on her own views – including how to behave and dress, and even who to date and marry. Mya continued to do as she was told until she could no longer cope and had a breakdown. She was in an unhappy relationship and didn't realize that she also had a voice and an opinion. She'd attracted a partner who kept her in the shadows, just as her mother had done. She was suppressed and didn't know who she was.

Mya was forced to stop working, and she became low in mood and anxious. However, she took this opportunity to undertake therapy, exploring her patterns and spending time understanding her life journey to date. She started to implement boundaries to keep herself safe, and found she was able to say 'no' to things without letting her guilt or the feeling that she was a bad person take over. It wasn't easy. She realized that she and her partner had different values and they ended the relationship; she also moved to a different city and started looking for a new job.

Mya realized that she had been living a life based on pleasing her mother and she broke free from this. It was beautiful to watch her journey unfold and to offer that safe space for her grow. Through the process Mya gained a new sense of identity and value and was able to live life as her true self. She learned she was enough and started living from this belief.

The Layer Cake of Suppressed Emotions

When we start digging through things, we unearth repressed feelings and desires. Speaking out and saying 'no' can initially feel overwhelming, especially with the emotions brought up by our increased understanding. I often have clients who say, 'But my childhood was amazing, and my parents gave me everything.' We sit with that for a while, and then we go deeper and deeper, uncovering layers of suppressed emotions.

Picture a beautiful sponge cake coated with icing. The cake looks perfect, decorative, and delicious. It is, as you've always understood it to be, a chocolate cake. All the other cakes you can see are chocolate cakes, so you're happy that this one is as well. But, when you grab a fork and decide to dive in, you realize it's only chocolate on the outside.

There are layers inside this cake – vanilla and peanut butter and raspberry – all pressed down and hidden beneath the chocolate. There are bits where the cake didn't quite cook perfectly, too. Yet the chocolate, which seemed so perfect, has covered them all.

As you release each layer, you learn something new about the cake. And, when you finally get down to the plate, you realize that the cake was something different, and much more complex, all along. Digging through the layers allowed you to reveal the cake's true nature, in all its messy, imperfect glory.

Just as digging through the cake revealed hidden layers, the searching you do through your own psyche will reveal parts of the self that have been suppressed or undeveloped, bringing them out to be nourished and to grow.

For example, shy people might discover a confidence they never knew they had, while people-pleasers awaken to values and aspirations that see their need for security and stability branch out in new directions. People who have been dominated by their emotions find themselves better able to stand back and be more objective and detached. Basically, this work enhances our sense of self and gives us the opportunity to explore new ways of meeting life.

The Power of Pause

In our fast-paced life journey, taking time away to think and plan may seem counterintuitive, a waste of the limited time we have. However, the value it brings in terms of gaining perspective, making strategic decisions, nurturing creativity, reducing stress, and setting future goals cannot be overstated.

> *By incorporating intentional pauses into our routines, we empower ourselves to navigate the challenges with greater clarity, purpose, and long-term success.*

When we're stuck on a problem, we often keep running through the same associations and options, but to no avail. By stepping away we engage other mental faculties and experience what are called 'incubation periods,' unconscious mental processes that aid in creative problem-solving. Scientists also describe this as 'beneficial forgetting.'[6] We can rewire our thinking, disconnect from unhelpful associations, and replace them with new, unique solutions, which is exactly what we want.

In the boundary-setting exercise for HFA Behavior Type 7, I suggested setting a timer and sitting with yourself to listen to your thoughts and feelings. This principle also applies here. And, by taking a few deep breaths alongside that pause, you'll provide your brain with the oxygen it needs to better engage with the executive function area.

To fund my master's degree, I had to work three jobs, and I remember I was constantly on the go; when I look back, I've no idea how I did it. I didn't give myself time to pause, because if I did, I'd have realized I was exhausted and stressed-out. I neglected my self-care and fell deeper into keeping myself busy.

However, my course involved having weekly therapy sessions, and this became my 'pause' space. I'd enter the therapy space with thousands of 'to do' things in my mind, yet the focus of that hour was on me, so I had to be present. If I wasn't, my therapist noticed. This taught me the power of pause. I became interested in breathwork, meditation, and other grounding techniques that have become key to the way I manage my well-being and mental health.

It's important to note that *pause* can look different to each of us. For some, it can be making a cup of tea or sitting outside without any technology and noticing the sounds around them, while for others it could be meditating. Whatever pause is for you, make it part of your lifestyle.

STEP 4 SUMMARY

We've reached the end of Step 4, so take a moment to reflect. How are you feeling about your journey so far? How have the steps, and the associated learning, changed things for you? Consider where you are and where you've come from. This is deep, powerful work, and you've done well to get this far.

Changes of a deep nature are occurring. You may feel as though everything is in upheaval or breaking apart, but it's more like the butterfly trying to free itself from the cocoon. It's time to question your upbringing, your beliefs, what you've been told all your life and tried to fit into. You're now in a space where you can think for yourself, a space that fits you instead. The great psychoanalyst Carl Jung said that 'meaning makes a great deal of things bearable – perhaps everything.' You're now finding your own meaning in life, your own acceptance of who you are, and it's immensely powerful.

It's important to note that when our belief system alters, our values also change as we become more conscious and intentional. And when our values change, the choices we make about how to lead our lives won't remain the same. This means our direction changes. Our vibration changes and so does who we attract. Just ignoring all this isn't going to work anymore. It's here, and it's knocking on your door. It's not going away, no matter how much you try to block it out. So, answer it. You don't have to let it in. You decide. Your choice. Are you ready for Step 5?

STEP 5

Unleash Self-Compassion

In the introduction, I explained why I chose to write this book. I said that I want people to feel good enough without having to seek validation from others, and to no longer struggle with their thoughts. I want to help people see that there's an opportunity to change, and that this change comes from within. I want to share my five-step plan so that you, and other people like you, can finally be free of the behavior patterns and limiting ways of thinking that hold you back.

It's been a real journey for you to reach this point in the book. It will have taken true honesty, facing up to your fears, and digging deep into your past, as well as dealing with all the emotions that brings. So, here we are at Step 5. This is where you'll learn about self-compassion. A *whole chapter* on learning to be kind to yourself? Yes! This is all about how we treat ourselves and show up for ourselves on a daily basis. It's time to stop going through life being so hard on yourself and trying to live up to expectations you've set based on what others must do to make you feel good enough!

This step will help to ground you, just as trees are grounded by their roots. Self-compassion is your roots, so let it grow. When I ask my clients if they speak to others in the same way they speak to themselves, they almost all say that they wouldn't dream of it. So why are we so unkind to ourselves? Why do we accept crumbs so readily while giving everyone else the loaf of bread? We also deserve the loaf of bread. The truth is this: what we feel we deserve is rooted in our self-worth.

> *Everyone's journey is different; this one is all about you. You can't be everything to everyone and nothing to yourself.*

Imagine your mind is a garden and your thoughts are the seeds. You get to choose what seeds you plant in your garden. You can plant seeds of positivity, love, and abundance rather than seeds of fear and shame. You can spend time taking care of everyone else's garden, or you can work on making your own garden beautiful and attracting other beautiful people into it. Ask yourself, what seeds are you going to plant? And how are you going to care for your garden?

Write Your Own Code for Living

As I said earlier, I believe that the journey of life is one where we love ourselves by showing up with compassion and simply letting ourselves 'be.' I also believe that we each have our own ethos and 'code for living' that's unique to us. Part of honoring that code is understanding *why* it's important to us, and that understanding only comes when we truly know ourselves. The work you've done over the course of this book will hopefully have helped you get closer to this understanding of self.

People get the code they live by from many different areas of human existence. Consider Stoicism, for example, whose followers use a system of philosophy that originated in ancient Greece as a blueprint for living their own lives. However, in Step 5 I'm inviting you to write your *own* code for living, based upon your *own* life experiences. Everything you've learned in this book will help you to go deeper into yourself and your own wisdom, so you can create a way of life that truly reflects who you are.

When you love yourself, you attract better. When you treat yourself a certain way, you're letting the universe know that's what you think you deserve. Everything starts with how you feel about yourself. So, choose to feel worthy, valuable, special, and deserving of the very best.

The Powers: 12 Ways You Can Thrive

In Step 3, you assembled a tool kit with which to face your fear and self-doubt, and now we're going to look at 12 'powers' you can use to seek compassion, self-love, and, ultimately, joy – it's possible to find all of these things once you have understanding. Some of the powers may not work for you, whereas others will. Remember that you're unique and your pathway to thriving is your own.

Power 1: Practice Mindfulness

Be fully present in this moment, for it holds the power to shape your reality. Embrace the beauty and depth of now, for it's here that true joy, growth, and connection reside.

Studies suggest that practicing mindfulness can help reduce stress, boost our attention and concentration, improve our mental and physical health, and even increase our happiness. Embracing the power of stillness is also a powerful antidote to perfectionism, providing a much-needed pause to reconnect with our true self. But how does it work?

The truth is that mindfulness works differently for each of us. It's a practice that's as unique as we are. It doesn't have to be sitting on a yoga mat in the outdoors listening to the birds – it can also be found in everyday actions such as making a cup of tea or washing our hands. Essentially, mindfulness is a tool we can all use, simply by paying attention to our thoughts, feelings, and senses (sight, hearing, taste, touch, and smell), so that we become fully aware of our environment.

Building our awareness of ourselves and our surroundings is a brilliant way to raise our positive vibrations. Don't let life pass you by – become aware.

Mindfulness can lead us to be more considerate and thoughtful, too – which makes us more likely to be kind and compassionate to others and ourselves.

I remember that when I first started practicing mindfulness, I thought it was a waste of time. However, once I found a space free from the distractions of my phone or my never-ending to-do list, I was able to listen to my self-talk and recognize the unrealistic standards that stemmed from my perfectionism and led to stress and anxiety. The pause helped me to understand which of my patterns were being fueled by fear.

Bringing your attention to the present can help you release your focus on the past and future which, in turn, can decrease your stress levels. By cultivating present-moment awareness and non-judgmental observation, we can break free from the grip of perfectionism. Ultimately, practicing mindfulness and embracing stillness empowers us to embrace our authentic selves, to find joy in the present moment, and to live with greater ease, balance, and fulfillment. It's in stillness that we embrace the beauty of being perfectly imperfect. Mindfulness works well when it's done with intention, so let's add some of that to your week with the following exercise.

MINDFUL INTENTION

Sit down and take the time to let yourself feel what you need to feel. Let it all out and breathe. Pause and connect with yourself. Visualize what you want to let go of. The present moment is the place for conscious change.

You can also practice mindfulness by keeping a gratitude journal, by walking in nature, meditating, noticing your feelings and emotions, and engaging in breathing exercises. You can do all these things at once, or you can try one each day. Starting a mindful practice requires just a 60-second commitment. And, whenever you *do* feel overwhelmed by your thoughts or a specific incident, you can ask yourself the following questions:

1. Am I overreacting? Is this really such a big deal? Is it important in the long run?

2. Am I overgeneralizing? Am I reaching a conclusion based more on opinion or experience than facts?

3. Am I mind-reading? Am I assuming others have specific beliefs or feel a certain way? Am I guessing how they'll react?

4. Am I labeling myself harshly? Am I referring to myself using words like 'stupid,' 'hopeless,' or 'fat?'

5. Is this an all-or-nothing thought? Am I viewing the incident as either good or bad without considering that reality is rarely black or white? The answer usually lies in the gray area between the two.

6. How truthful and accurate is this thought? Can I step back and consider things the way a friend or an impartial observer might? Be objective rather than subjective?

Power 2: Pay Attention to Your Inner Dialogue

Listen closely to the whispers of your inner voice, for within them lie the seeds of self-belief, empowerment, and transformation. Nurture your self-talk with kindness, encouragement, and compassion, and watch as it blossoms into a powerful force that propels you toward your dreams.

By developing your self-awareness and learning how to listen to the way you speak to yourself, you can cultivate a compassionate and empowering inner dialogue. Tuning in to our inner voice has a profound impact on how we show up in the world, and we gain a deeper understanding of our desires, fears, strengths, and limitations.

This self-awareness allows us to make conscious choices and align our actions with our authentic self. We no longer feel compelled to conform to societal expectations or wear masks to please others. Instead, we embrace our uniqueness and confidently express our genuine thoughts and emotions.

Moreover, when we listen to ourselves, we become more attuned to our intuition and inner wisdom. And by trusting our intuition, we navigate life with a greater sense of purpose and direction, guided by our own internal compass. By honoring our needs and taking proactive steps to meet them, we cultivate a healthier relationship with ourselves. This self-care extends beyond our personal well-being and impacts how we engage with others. When we prioritize our own well-being, we have more energy, compassion, and presence to offer to the world.

Your thoughts are the source of your emotions and moods. The conversations you have with yourself can be destructive or beneficial, influencing how you feel about yourself and how you respond to events in your life. We can learn a lot when we tune in and listen to how we speak to ourselves. We become aware of self-limiting beliefs, negative self-talk, and patterns that no longer serve us. With this self-awareness, we can challenge and reframe those limiting narratives, empowering ourselves to embrace new possibilities and expand our horizons.

> *By listening to our inner voice, we open*
> *ourselves up to learning, adapting, and*
> *evolving into the best version of ourselves.*

Every experience can be an opportunity for research and development – if you take the time to listen. Remember, this is an ongoing journey. Self-talk operates in the same way as any relationship; it requires time and focus. There will be times where things don't go to plan and you end up getting frustrated or annoyed with yourself, but in that moment you have a choice: to understand yourself or to bully yourself.

What I've found with myself and other people I've worked with is that often we're afraid to stop 'bullying' as we don't think we'll get things done any other way. We become used to doing things through fear motivation. So, let's try the opposite: doing things with intention and alignment. If we look at the two sides of self-talk, we can see how one is negative and the other is supportive and affirming. Consider the following two statements, and then say them out loud to yourself.

1. 'I'm going to speak up in the meeting today because I have something important to contribute.'

2. 'I don't think I want to speak up in the meeting today because I'll look foolish or stupid if I say the wrong thing.'

Notice how you feel after you say each one. Statement 1 can leave you feeling empowered, while statement 2 can make you feel like a turtle who wants to go back into its shell. By paying attention to your inner dialogue, you can develop a greater sense of self-connection and authenticity. This practice also enhances your ability to respond consciously to situations rather than react impulsively based on automatic thoughts.

CHALLENGE YOUR SELF-TALK

Take a moment to think about what you've said to yourself today. Was it critical, or was it kind and helpful? How did you feel after you engaged in this inner discussion? Did you speak to yourself in the same way you'd speak to a friend? Consider the following statements and the positive alternatives. Which are most representative of the way you speak to yourself?

- 'What an idiot! I really screwed up that presentation. Well, that's the end of my career.' *Alternative*: 'I can do better than that. I'll prepare and rehearse more next time. Maybe I'll get some public-speaking training. That would be good for my career.'

- 'I can't do that in just one week. It's impossible.' *Alternative*: 'It's a lot to do, but I'll take it one step at a time. I think I'll see if my friends can help, too.'

- 'How ridiculous! I can't teach myself how to think more positively.' *Alternative*: 'Learning to think more positively can help me in many ways. I'm going to give it a go.'

- 'I look so fat in this dress. No wonder I can't get a date. Why can't

I lose weight? What's wrong with me?' *Alternative*: 'I'm beautiful just as I am, and there's nothing wrong with me. I'm happy, I'm healthy, and I'm loved.'

How did it go? If you find that your inner thoughts tend to skew toward the negative statements, it's time to switch gears and learn a new approach to self-talk. Next time you tell yourself something negative, I challenge you to stop and reword what you said in a kinder, more positive light, as in the alternative statements shown here. Repeat as often as it takes. Carry your light forward.

Power 3: Let Yourself Shine

Embrace the luminosity within you and let it radiate. It's far better to stand boldly in your own light than diminish yourself to conform with the shadows of others.

Stop striving for validation. Don't compromise your authenticity in order to conform. You are enough. Give your time to people who are revitalizing and emotionally prepared for deep connection. This doesn't mean you must disconnect from everyone who doesn't make you feel a certain way. That's not how relationships work. Instead, discover what it is that they trigger in you, and then see if there's space to navigate through this with them, as this can deepen your relationship.

Preserve the radiance of your true self and resist the urge to shrink in order to please others. When you notice that you feel the need to change yourself when you're with a particular person, this is a great insight for internal growth. It may be the result of something that's coming up for you, so it's an opportunity to learn more about yourself and why you act the way you do. Every day can bring us a new opportunity to gain further insight, helping us to evolve.

Don't betray yourself by continuing patterns in which you feel you need to put everyone else first. You need to understand why you do this, and what need it serves. However, understanding alone won't lead to change. You must do the work as well, and that takes practice. Reading this book is a great start!

It's more powerful to shine as your true self than to dim your light to fit in with others. Your uniqueness and individuality are what make you extraordinary.

I've found that when we talk about true self and authentic self, it's about integrating the part of us that comes from our HFA (the high-functioning part) and the part of us that we've never nurtured before but are starting to. By this I mean that finding your true self doesn't mean eliminating your HFA. If anything, I'd say that it involves embracing it as part of you, using the insights HFA gives you into how sensitively you connect with others and the world around you. The key is to no longer let HFA control you.

For example, in the past my HFA would be my dominant self. Now, however, if someone asks me to do something that I can't do, instead of saying 'yes' out of fear of upsetting them, I *notice* the fear. I can also then look objectively at my situation and not feel bad about letting the person know I can't help them right now because I have a lot on my own plate. I have space to regulate my fear rather than letting it drive me.

By honoring and expressing your true essence, you help create a world where authenticity is celebrated, and diversity thrives. Embrace your light and let it radiate, illuminating the path for others to shine brightly in their own right.

HONOR YOUR TRUE SELF

Whenever you notice that you're putting others on a pedestal and dimming your light due to feelings of being 'too much,' here are some helpful questions to ask yourself:

- What's the belief or thought pattern underlying my tendency to put others on a pedestal and to dim my light? How does this belief limit my self-expression and authenticity?

- What evidence do I have to support the idea that I'm too much? Are there specific situations or experiences that have contributed to this belief?

- How does dimming my light impact my overall well-being and sense of fulfillment?

- What are the unique strengths or qualities that I bring to the world?

- How might expressing my true self positively impact my relationships with others?

- What would it feel like to fully embrace my authentic self without the fear of being too much?

- How can I reframe my perspective to see my uniqueness as a gift rather than a burden?

- What steps can I take to honor my true self, keep shining my light, and sit with the discomfort this can bring?

By answering these questions, you can gain clarity on the underlying beliefs and patterns that contribute to you dimming your light. Through self-reflection and self-compassion, you can challenge these beliefs and develop strategies to embrace and express your true self, allowing yourself to shine unapologetically.

Power 4: Direct Your Energy Intentionally

Your energy is a precious resource. Consciously choose how and where you invest it. Direct it deliberately toward what truly matters to you, for it's when you align your energy with your passions and values that you unlock your full potential.

Imagine that you have only 100 units of energy available to you each day. How you choose to 'spend' them can significantly impact your overall well-being, productivity, and fulfillment. Choosing to spend your energy wisely, rather than using it to please others, is part of your healing and growth process. As the author and social justice activist L.R. Knost says, 'Taking care of myself doesn't mean "me first"– it means "me too".'

Remember, you hold the power to decide where your energy flows. So, embrace the gift of intentionality and direct it toward endeavors that uplift your spirit, align with your values, and ignite your passions.

By consciously choosing where your energy goes,
you create a life that is vibrant, purposeful,
and in harmony with your truest self.

When we expend our energy on things that don't align with our values, passions, or growth, we risk depleting ourselves emotionally, mentally, and even physically. We may find ourselves drained and disheartened, wondering why we lack the enthusiasm or motivation to pursue our dreams; or, worse still, believing that something's wrong with us. It's at this moment that we need to pause and reassess our energy investments.

Another way to look at it is as if you're painting a picture. Every decision you make about what you choose to do is another stroke of the brush. Are you painting a picture that makes you happy and reflects your true self? Or are you painting something derivative, based on what you think other people want? Be the artist, take control and shape your reality with each stroke of the brush, until you've created something that makes you happy.

As you become intentional about where your energy goes, you may find that certain aspects of your life require adjustment. Be compassionate with yourself during this process. Remember that change is a gradual journey, and each small shift is a step toward greater alignment and fulfillment. And it begins with self-awareness. Ask yourself: *Where's my energy going? Am I investing it wisely or am I squandering it in places that don't serve me?* The following exercise will help you direct your energy toward what truly brings you joy, passion, and a sense of purpose rather than what drains or depletes you.

IDENTIFY WHERE YOUR ENERGY GOES

In your journal or a notebook, create two columns labeled 'Energy Drainers' and 'Energy Boosters.' Then write down the activities, tasks, and interactions you experience during the day and categorize them as either a drainer or a booster.

- **Energy Drainers:** Activities or interactions that leave you feeling drained, depressed, or depleted. These might include tasks you don't enjoy, engaging in gossip or negativity, or spending time with people who sap your energy.

- **Energy Boosters:** Activities or interactions that leave you feeling energized, fulfilled, and joyful. These might include favorite hobbies, spending time with loved ones, engaging in creative pursuits, or moments of relaxation and self-care.

After a few days of journaling, review your entries and notice any patterns that emerge. Are there specific activities or interactions that consistently drain your energy? Are there certain activities that consistently boost your energy and mood?

With this newfound awareness, set intentions for the following day or week. Aim to reduce or limit energy-draining activities and prioritize energy-boosting ones. Be realistic and gentle with yourself, recognizing that small changes can have a significant impact over time.

As you go about your day, practice mindfulness when making choices about where to allocate your time and energy. Before engaging in an activity or interaction, pause for a moment and check in with yourself. Ask, *Will this activity boost or drain my energy? Does it align with my values and priorities?*

Acknowledge and celebrate the positive shifts you make in how you direct your energy. Be patient with yourself as you continue to refine your choices, knowing that mindful awareness and practice will lead to lasting change.

Here's another exercise for learning to direct your energy.

THE WHEEL OF LIFE

In a notebook, draw the Wheel of Life diagram shown below. Review the eight category segments given and, if necessary, rename them to include a category that's missing, or to make the wheel more meaningful to you. Next, draw a line across each category segment, scoring it between 1 (very dissatisfied) and 10 (fully satisfied).

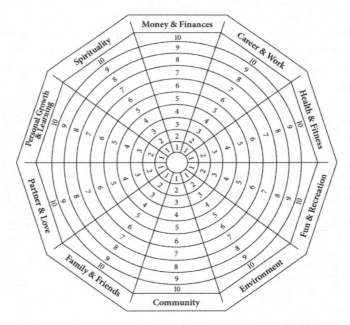

The Wheel of Life

Make some time to sit with your Wheel of Life and ask yourself honestly how you feel about each 'segment' of your life. This will give you food for thought about how or what you would like to change.

The Wheel of Life is powerful because it provides a visual representation of key areas of your life, and a holistic view of your current state of well-being and balance. It allows you to identify areas where you might be dedicating too much time and energy, while neglecting other important aspects. Because imbalances can lead to stress, burnout, and decreased well-being, I encourage you to revisit the Wheel of Life monthly, to help you visualize the imbalances in your life and, ultimately, the power and possibility of implementing change.

Power 5: Appreciate Your True Self

Amid the symphony of souls, find your distinctive note and play it boldly.

In a world that often glorifies conformity, it takes courage to embrace our uniqueness and appreciate our differences. A journey of self-discovery and self-acceptance requires us to explore the depths of our being, shedding the masks of societal expectations and comparison to others. It's when we honor our authentic self that we truly find a sense of belonging and fulfillment.

It's time to finally let go of the idea of 'perfect' and comparing yourself to others and welcome your uniqueness. You've gone through this process already in earlier steps – learning how an endless struggle to appear 'perfect' can only lead to exhaustion and burnout because perfect doesn't exist. Embracing our imperfections allows us to recognize that they aren't flaws but the brushstrokes that make our canvas unique and remarkable.

By transcending the illusion of perfection, confronting your fears, and navigating your HFA, you'll reveal the true essence of who you really are – a mosaic of brilliance and resilience.

I found it very difficult to appreciate my differences and to accept the compliments that others gave me for being me. I was so quick to put everyone else on a pedestal and appreciate how brilliant *they* were, yet I found this almost impossible to do for myself. One thing I will say is keep practicing! Don't give up.

In the vast tapestry of humanity, no two threads are exactly the same. Each of us is a masterpiece woven with unique colors, patterns, and textures. Accepting our individuality and valuing the differences that make us who we are is a powerful part of the human experience. In a world that seems to yearn for authenticity and acceptance, embracing your uniqueness and appreciating the differences of others is an act of courage and love.

Embrace and appreciate the wonderful things that make you, you. Explore yourself, your joys and sorrows, your talents, and desires, whatever it is that makes you tick. And revel in the feeling that you're wonderful and unique. You're the books you read, the movies you watch, the music you listen to, the people you spend time with, the conversions you engage in. Choose wisely what you feed your mind.

We also need to remember to be gentle with ourselves, acknowledging that growth is a process and setbacks are stepping stones to progress. There will be times when you'll want to fall back into old patterns, limiting yourself in a bid to feel that you 'belong.' Self-compassion will help you navigate these inevitable setbacks with grace, promoting resilience and a deeper relationship with yourself and others. Accept your uniqueness, cherish your journey, and let the authentic beauty of your soul illuminate the world with a radiance that only you can bring.

MIRROR AFFIRMATIONS

Stand in front of a mirror and take a few deep breaths to center yourself. Look into your eyes and say out loud three positive affirmations about yourself that celebrate your uniqueness and differences. Here are some examples:

- 'I'm unique and I accept myself for who I am.'

- 'I embrace my quirks and relish my individuality.'

- 'I'm worthy of love and acceptance just as I am.'

Repeat these mirror affirmations daily for a week. Notice any shifts in your self-perception and how the words influence your outlook on your own uniqueness and differences. This simple practice can help build self-appreciation and foster a deeper sense of acceptance of your true self.

Power 6: Notice the Stories You Tell Yourself

In the theater of our mind, the stories we tell ourselves take center stage. As both playwright and protagonist, we compose a narrative that can either confine us to the shadows of doubt or propel us into the spotlight of self-discovery and empowerment. Embrace the art of conscious storytelling, for it's in rewriting our inner scripts that we uncover the true potential of our heart and mind.

We've spoken already about catastrophizing, of imagining the worst and telling ourselves lies that hold us back. The mind is a masterful storyteller, weaving intricate narratives about who we are, what we can achieve, and how the world perceives us. The 'what if' this happens or 'what if' that happens – as you've learned, HFA takes us down the Rabbit Hole of Doom, and it can be difficult to get out.

The stories we tell ourselves, which are born from our beliefs, experiences, and interpretations, influence every aspect of our lives and shape how we show up in the world. If we perceive ourselves as capable, deserving, and resilient, we'll approach challenges with confidence. Conversely, if we harbor self-doubt, unworthiness, or fear, we may hold back, hesitating to seize opportunities and navigate the unknown.

The stories we tell ourselves often emerge from a place of protection, guarding us against the feelings stirred up by challenges, rejections, or moments of vulnerability. We create these stories to offer explanations for our shortcomings, fears, or past mistakes, making it easier to cope with life's complexities and shielding us from hurt and disappointment.

But blaming all your emotions on events and people outside of you creates a situation where you're constantly giving away your power. Taking responsibility for your mindset not only helps you grow, but it also widens your opportunity for happiness. And it allows you to take back that power.

While the protective stories you tell yourself may serve a purpose initially, they can eventually become anchors that weigh you down. To break free from their constraints, you need to develop a conscious awareness of them and their impact on your life. It's time to rewrite your endless catastrophes into something positive.

> *Remember, you're the author of your own story, capable of transforming self-limiting tales into empowering sagas that lead you to the fullest expression of yourself.*

Practice bringing yourself back to the present moment, especially when your mind is focusing too much on the past and future, or on what 'might happen.' Being able to re-center yourself so you don't jump to conclusions can help stop you from acting rashly, or from not acting at all.

Challenge your limiting beliefs, question their validity, and open yourself to new possibilities. Rewrite your stories with growth-oriented themes. For example, *I'm resilient and capable of learning from setbacks. I deserve success and happiness. I have unique gifts that can positively impact the world.*

TAKE A REALITY CHECK

This five-part exercise is designed to help you challenge the validity of the stories you tell yourself and bring a sense of objectivity to your thoughts. By asking specific reality check questions, you can gain clarity about the accuracy of your inner narratives.

1: Identify the Story

When you notice a particular story or thought pattern surfacing, pause, and identify the main theme or belief behind it. For example, if the story is *I'll never succeed in my career*, the underlying belief might be *I'm not good enough*.

2: Ask Your Reality Check Questions

- *Is this story based on facts or assumptions?* Consider whether there's tangible evidence to support the story or if it's built on unfounded assumptions or past experiences.

- *What's the worst-case scenario?* Imagine the worst outcome if the story were true. Often, you'll realize that the imagined consequences are unlikely or manageable.

- *What evidence contradicts the story?* List any past achievements, positive feedback, or instances where the story's been proven wrong.

- *How would I advise a friend?* Imagine a close friend sharing a similar story. What advice would you offer them? Apply that same advice to yourself.

- *What's a more balanced perspective?* Try to find a more balanced view of the situation by considering both positive and negative aspects.

3: Create a New Perspective

After answering the reality check questions, write down a more balanced and empowering perspective to counter the limiting story. For example, *While I may face challenges, I've overcome obstacles in the past and have the skills to navigate through them.*

4: Reframe the Story

Take your more balanced and empowering new perspective and transform it into an affirmation or positive statement. Repeat this affirmation/statement whenever the old limiting story resurfaces.

5: Practice Mindful Awareness

Throughout the day, pay attention to your thoughts and emotions. Whenever you catch yourself falling into a limiting story, gently bring your awareness back to the reality check questions and the new perspective you've created.

By consistently practicing this reality check exercise, you become more aware of the stories you tell yourself and can challenge them with objectivity and compassion. Over time, you'll gain greater control over your thought patterns, leading to a reduced sense of fear and anxiety and a more positive and empowering mindset.

Power 7: Set Realistic Expectations

Unlock the power of boundaries to liberate yourself from the burden of over-responsibility and the whirlwind of our busy culture. Set yourself free and discover the beauty of balance, reclaiming the essence of your own being.

While ambition and determination can be positive traits, when they're coupled with unrealistic expectations, they can become a recipe for exhaustion and burnout. With HFA, the pressure to excel in every aspect of life can be overwhelming, pushing us to stretch beyond our limits and neglect our well-being.

While you might have your goals, be aware that you can work toward them without breaking yourself in the process. There's nothing valiant about burnout. Instead, use your energy intentionally and put in good work toward the things you love, doing them in a balanced way. In the pursuit of excellence, true success lies not in stretching beyond your limits but in nurturing your well-being.

Embrace your goals with intention, for there's strength in acknowledging that greatness thrives in balance, not at the expense of your own self.

In the past, our HFA might have led us to push ourselves to meet unattainable benchmarks. However, as this book has shown you, chasing perfection usually leads to a sense of inadequacy and a deep-seated fear of failure. This fear then drives us to work longer hours, sacrifice our leisure time, and overlook self-care as we go after our goals. The cycle of overcommitment and neglect often leads to feelings of resentment toward others who seem to balance it all effortlessly.

Learning to set realistic standards and manage your energy more effectively will help you to relinquish those unrealistic expectations, liberating you from a heavy burden that stifles your joy and well-being.

I remember the process of transitioning into a space where I was being kinder to myself. At first, I felt disgust when I spoke compassionately to myself, as I'd only ever been hard on myself. However, in time, I found that adopting a mindset of self-compassion and setting realistic expectations created a harmonious balance in my life. As I learned to appreciate myself and my journey, the biggest thing I discovered was that true fulfillment comes from being authentic, present, and whole.

Letting go of the heavy weight of unrealistic expectations frees us to forge a path toward genuine happiness, self-acceptance, and inner peace. By honoring our limitations and setting achievable goals, we unlock our potential to move toward living a purposeful and contented life.

MINDFUL DAILY LIVING

Use the following exercise to help guide you through different experiences. For example, when a colleague asks you to do some work for them, you can tell them you'll check your own workload first and get back to them, rather than saying 'yes' right away. This will buy you some time to process the request and go through the following six prompts:

1: Reflect on Your Values

Take some time to identify your core values. What truly matters to you in life? Understanding your values will guide you in setting goals that align with your authentic self. *In the example above:* If agreeing to do the extra work means you must miss a gym session and stay up later, consider which option is more important to you.

2: Identify Your Priorities

With a clear understanding of your core values, write down your top priorities. These are the areas of life that deserve your focus and attention. *In the example:* You know that if you miss the gym session it will impact your mood. Plus, you won't have time to cook dinner, which means you'll have to get take-out, adding further to the negative spiral in your mood. You're also meant to meet with friends for drinks tomorrow and don't want to cancel as it's been in the diary for months.

3: Practice Self-Compassion

Be gentle with yourself when setbacks occur. Having realistic expectations acknowledges that setbacks are part of the process, so treat yourself with the same kindness you would offer to a friend. *In the example:* You might feel bad for saying 'no' to your colleague, but also know that what they're asking of you isn't part of your workload, and therefore it's not something you *have* to do.

4: Say 'No' When Necessary

Recognize that saying 'no' to certain commitments or requests doesn't make you selfish. It's essential to protect your time and energy to pursue what truly matters. *In the example:* You let your colleague know that you've looked at your schedule but can't accommodate the extra work, so you're unable to accept it. You do this without feeling guilty about it.

5: Create Boundaries

Establish healthy boundaries in your personal and professional life. Know when to take breaks, and ensure you have time for self-care and relaxation. *In the example:* This isn't the first time you've been asked to take on extra work by this colleague, and you've said 'yes' on most occasions. Now you must learn the hard lesson that, while you might want to be kind, you also must teach people how you want to be treated. Setting a boundary by saying 'no' is part of this process.

6: Reassess and Adjust

Life's fluid, and circumstances change. Periodically reassess your goals and expectations, making adjustments as necessary to stay aligned with your evolving reality. *In the example:* You might feel proud but also guilty about setting this initial boundary. Yet you know it's the right thing to do, so you acknowledge your guilt and don't allow it to drag you back into old patterns of people-pleasing.

Power 8: Create Gratitude Moments

Carve out precious pockets of gratitude amid life's demands, where you can cherish the present, honor the past, and embrace the abundance that surrounds you.

For high-functioning perfectionists, the quest for excellence can become all-consuming, leaving little room for self-care and appreciation of life's blessings. It's easy to get swept away by the pressure of the next thing you need to do and all your responsibilities, while forgetting to take a moment to breathe and appreciate all that surrounds you.

Creating a gratitude moment means intentionally setting aside time each day to cultivate a deep sense of appreciation and self-reflection. It's a powerful practice that allows you to tap into the transformative power of gratitude, reminding you of the countless blessings in your life, big and small. Whether it's savoring the warmth of the morning sun, relishing a heartfelt conversation, or cherishing the simple pleasure of a hot drink or a soft jumper, these moments ground us in the present, nurturing our connection to ourselves, others, and the world around us.

Through these moments of self-reflection, we become attuned to the richness of our experiences, fostering a profound sense of contentment, joy, and a deeper appreciation for the journey we're on. This then leads to a shift in our perspective. We begin to appreciate the journey of growth rather than fixate on any perceived failures, creating a harmonious balance between ambition and contentment and treating ourselves with compassion.

True fulfillment lies not only in our achievements but also in cherishing the beauty of the present moment and embracing our true self.

Don't keep striving for the next thing. Stop and PAUSE. Remember, the goal isn't to ignore life's challenges but to reframe your perspective and foster a greater sense of gratitude for the positives. Carving out gratitude moments is a gentle reminder to slow down, savor the goodness in life, and nurture a grateful heart. Reflecting on all the beautiful and simple things around you that are often taken for granted will help ground you. Being able to remember all the good things and people in your life stops the mind from solely focusing on what it wants next. It's easy to flow between gratitude and joy.

GRATITUDE JOURNALING

One way to cultivate gratitude is through journaling. Find a quiet and comfortable space where you can reflect without distractions, and follow these steps:

1: Set Aside Time

Choose a specific time each day to dedicate to your gratitude practice. It can be in the morning, before bed, or during a break. You can even schedule it in your diary so you can get reminders.

2: Reflect on Three Blessings

Ask yourself, *Which three things that happened today am I grateful for?* They can be big or small, personal or general; it doesn't matter, as long as they mean something to you. Then ask, *Why am I grateful for these three things?* This question will lead you deeper into the 'why' and give you the space to process. The more you do this, the more you train your mind to look out for the wonder in everyday life.

3: Feel the Gratitude

As you think about or write down your three blessings, immerse yourself in the feelings of gratitude for each one. Allow yourself to fully experience the positive emotions associated with them.

4: Repeat Daily

Make this gratitude journaling exercise a daily practice. Consistency is key when rewiring your brain to naturally focus on the positives in your life.

5: Explore New Perspectives

Even during the most difficult experiences, challenge yourself to find gratitude in these situations or unexpected places. This can help shift your mindset and promote resilience.

6: Review and Reflect

Regularly review your gratitude journal entries. Notice patterns, growth, and changes in your perspective over time. Use this self-reflection to further deepen your appreciation for life's gifts. You could even try journaling with your partner, children, and friends.

Power 9: Avoid Comparing Yourself to Others

As Theodore Roosevelt once said, comparison is the thief of joy. Embrace your own journey, for it's uniquely yours, and therein lies your true strength and beauty.

We often catch ourselves peeking through the window of other people's lives, wondering why we don't have what they have or why we aren't achieving what they've achieved. The seed of self-doubt takes root, and we start questioning our worth and capabilities. But read that again. I said, 'peeking through the window,' meaning we only ever see a snapshot. Comparing our life to a snapshot of someone else's is just not realistic.

Comparison is a natural human tendency, but it's essential to learn how to manage it and redirect your focus to your own growth and well-being. Embracing your uniqueness and valuing your journey will lead to greater self-acceptance, contentment, and a more fulfilling life. The truth is that you aren't meant to be a copy of someone else; you're meant to be uniquely you. Embracing your journey without comparing yourself to others means honoring your individuality and recognizing the beauty in your own story. It's about acknowledging and accepting that your path is your own and will always be different from everyone else's. That's precisely what makes it extraordinary.

When you let go of the measuring stick and free yourself from the constraints of comparison, you also free yourself from the weight of unrealistic expectations. Trust that every twist and turn of your messy, imperfect, wonderful journey is leading you exactly where you need to be.

As you embrace your journey, you discover
that the true magic of life lies not in being like
others but in authentically being yourself.

Remember, your worth isn't determined by how you measure up to others. I realize that breaking the habit of comparison takes time and patience, but once you get on the path of self-acceptance and self-compassion, it will lead you to a more fulfilling and authentic life. Your path is yours alone to walk, so honor your uniqueness and let go of the need to compare. Be inspired by others but never defined by them. Embrace your distinctive path, for it's the key to unlocking the limitless potential within you.

MANAGE YOUR COMPARISON THOUGHTS

This exercise is intended for daily practice. Use it to help you identify where you compare yourself or your life to others. Pay attention to situations, environments, or people that trigger self-comparisons. Becoming aware of your triggers helps you anticipate when you might fall into the comparison trap.

1: Pause and Acknowledge

When you catch yourself comparing, pause for a moment. Acknowledge the comparison without judgment. Remember that it's normal for the mind to make comparisons, but doing so doesn't define your worth or value.

2: Challenge Negative Thoughts

Challenge the negative thoughts that arise during comparison. Ask yourself if these thoughts are based on realistic expectations or if they're driven by social pressures or insecurities.

3: Reframe and Redirect

Reframe your comparison thoughts using positive and empowering statements. Remind yourself of your own unique qualities and accomplishments. Embrace the idea that everyone's journey is different, and that this is what makes life beautiful and diverse.

4: Cultivate Self-Compassion

Be kind and compassionate toward yourself. Treat yourself as you would a dear friend who's struggling with self-comparison. Practice self-compassion and remind yourself that it's okay to be imperfect and to have your own path in life.

Power 10: Unlock Self-Trust

Self-trust is the anchor of inner strength, guiding you through the waves of uncertainty with confidence and resilience.

Self-trust is a steadfast belief in your abilities, decisions, and worth – when you believe in and trust yourself, you can navigate life with confidence and authenticity. HFA can often entangle us in a web of worry and self-doubt, making it difficult to find peace, but self-trust will help you break free from this. Once you recognize your capabilities and acknowledge your fears, you'll be able to trust your instincts without seeking reassurance from others.

Self-trust doesn't mean having blind confidence in every aspect of your life; rather, it involves a healthy acceptance of your vulnerability and growth.

> *By acknowledging that mistakes are natural and setbacks are opportunities to learn, we become able to forgive ourselves.*

Remember my client who kept a mental file of all her perceived failures? Self-trust will allow you to throw away your own file and be kind to yourself. You won't succeed at everything you try, but a strong sense of self-belief means you'll at least give things a try, rather than holding yourself back.

At the heart of self-trust lies a deep acceptance of who we are. When we trust ourselves, we recognize that our worth isn't contingent on others' opinions or the attainment of perfection. This liberates us from the shackles of comparison and self-doubt, allowing us to enjoy our uniqueness without reservation. We become more capable of handling whatever life throws our way, carrying a deeper sense of self-reliance and emotional stability.

Like any skill, self-trust can be learned through regular self-reflection and conscious effort. Start by listening to your intuition and honoring your feelings and needs. Celebrate your accomplishments, no matter how small, and remind yourself of the challenges you've already overcome. Remember, this is a new way of being. It may feel strange at first, almost as though you're boasting in some way, but all you're doing is acknowledging that *you are enough.*

The relentless pursuit of perfection and our fear of failure can trap us in a cycle of self-criticism and overachievement. However, by trusting ourselves, we can free ourselves from the grip of anxiety and the need for external validation. We can learn to regard our mistakes and setbacks as stepping stones to progress, fostering resilience and emotional well-being.

This fearlessness opens doors to new opportunities and experiences, propelling us beyond our comfort zone and toward growth and self-discovery. Embrace the power of self-trust, and you'll find yourself journeying through life with unwavering confidence and an open heart, ready to face all that comes your way. The following quick and simple exercise will help reinforce self-trust and build your confidence in your abilities.

SELF-TRUST AFFIRMATIONS

Close your eyes and take a deep breath, inhaling through the nose and exhaling through the mouth. Allow yourself to relax and let go of any tension. Repeat positive self-trust affirmations to yourself silently or out loud. Choose wording that resonates with you; here are some examples:

- 'I trust myself and my decisions.'

- 'I believe in my abilities and embrace my uniqueness.'

- 'I'm enough, just as I am.'

- 'I'm capable of handling any challenges that come my way.'

By consistently repeating these affirmations, you'll strengthen your self-trust and cultivate a greater sense of belief in your abilities. Over time, you'll find that your self-doubt and insecurities diminish, and you'll face life's challenges with a newfound sense of assurance and resilience.

Power 11: Live Courageously and Be Vulnerable

Courageous living is the art of embracing our vulnerability, for it's in our openness that we discover the true strength within.

Being vulnerable is often misunderstood as an invitation to bare our souls to everyone we encounter. However, true vulnerability isn't about indiscriminately sharing every aspect of ourselves;

rather, it's the courageous act of opening our hearts to those we deem worthy of holding our most tender truths.

You need only one skill for wholehearted living, and that's the courage to be vulnerable. Brené Brown has written about the importance of this and in her research and work, she emphasizes the importance of embracing vulnerability as a key component of living a fulfilling and authentic life.[7] Brown believes that vulnerability isn't a weakness; rather, it's a strength, as it allows us to connect with others, show our true selves, and experience deeper emotions and relationships.

Being truly vulnerable means striking a balance between revealing our authentic selves and setting boundaries to protect our emotional well-being. Remember, vulnerability is a testament to our strength – the strength to acknowledge our imperfections, fears, and insecurities without judgment or shame.

It might be difficult to do at first, but with practice we can learn that it's okay to be vulnerable and trust our ability to stay in that space even when things around us feel uncertain. We also learn to trust the people around us, especially those who prove themselves to be safe havens for our vulnerabilities. Hold on to these people, for they're the ones with whom you can share your deepest self, knowing they'll hold you with compassion and without judgment. See if you can be that person for them, as well.

It's through our vulnerability that we forge genuine bonds with others, allowing our authentic selves to be seen and known.

Embracing our vulnerability isn't a one-time decision; it's an ongoing journey of self-discovery and growth. As we dare to be vulnerable, dare to expose our heart's desires, we reclaim our power and authenticity. We learn that being vulnerable isn't about seeking validation or approval from others; it's about finding strength in our deepest self in the face of life's uncertainties.

DELVE INTO YOUR VULNERABILITY

This exercise will help you to look at your vulnerability, build your courage, and deepen your understanding of your emotions and experiences.

1: Reflect on Past Experiences

Think about the times in your life when you felt vulnerable. It could be when you took a risk, shared your feelings, or faced a difficult situation. Write down these experiences in your journal or on a piece of paper.

2: Explore Your Emotions

For each vulnerable experience, explore the emotions you felt at that time. Were you scared, anxious, excited, or hopeful? Acknowledge and name these emotions without judgment.

3: Identify Triggers

Reflect on what triggered your vulnerability in each situation. Was it the fear of judgment, rejection, or failure? Identifying the triggers will help you understand which aspects of vulnerability are most challenging for you.

4: Practice Self-Compassion

As you explore your vulnerability, be gentle with yourself. Practice self-compassion by acknowledging that vulnerability is a natural part of being human and that it's okay to feel these emotions.

5: Visualize Courageous Responses

Now, visualize how you would have responded in those vulnerable situations with even more courage. Imagine expressing yourself authentically and embracing your vulnerability without holding back.

6: Journal Your Insights

Write down your reflections, insights, and any new perspectives you've gained from completing this exercise. Consider what you've learned about yourself and your relationship with vulnerability.

7: Set Small Challenges for the Future

Take small steps toward being more courageous with vulnerability in your daily life. It could be initiating a heartfelt conversation, sharing your creative work, or asking for support when you need it. Reflect and journal on how you feel when you do this.

Power 12: Practice Patience

Patience isn't passive waiting; rather, it's a skill that helps you navigate life's currents with grace, embracing the journey of growth one step at a time.

This was probably the hardest power for me to learn. I remember watching *Star Wars* and being struck by how irritated Luke

Skywalker was, wanting answers from Yoda when none were forthcoming. However, just like the Jedi in *Star Wars*, we too must learn the art of patience. In our pursuit of change, we may initially overlook how significant patience can be, instead seeking quick results and immediate success. But it's in patience that we discover the true essence of growth. As we persist with patience, we unveil the hidden power within ourselves, transforming into masters of our own destiny. In this world of instant gratification, the virtue of patience emerges as a profound source of strength and wisdom.

> *At its core, patience is a testament to self-trust and an affirmation of our journey. It reminds us that growth is a gradual process and that great transformations unfold in their own time.*

In moments of impatience, we risk succumbing to self-doubt and frustration, overlooking the beauty of each step in our personal evolution. The pressure to excel and fear of failure can drive us to push ourselves beyond our limits. However, practicing patience gives us the space to be with our thoughts, to regulate what's going on inside before jumping into things that don't feel right for us. Instead, we embrace the wisdom of pacing ourselves.

Practicing patience also strengthens how we relate to others, fostering deeper connections and understanding. Instead of being impatient with people when things aren't happening as we think they should, we relax, and let things happen in their own time. By actively listening and allowing others the space to express themselves, we nurture empathy and compassion.

Patience opens the door to heartfelt communication and helps us to build bridges of trust between ourselves and others. This is so important, as HFA can make it difficult for us to trust others. Patience is part of the process of learning to be kind – not only to others but also to ourselves. However, like each of the other 'powers,' cultivating patience takes work. Mindfulness practices, such as meditation and deep breathing, are helpful when it comes to remaining anchored in the present moment. Regular self-reflection is also useful, as it gives us space to make sure we aren't rushing things or pushing too hard. Patience allows us to breathe.

MINDFUL BREATH FOR PATIENCE

This quick and effective exercise will help you cultivate patience and find tranquility whenever you feel restless.

1: Count Your Breaths

Sit or stand in a relaxed posture, with your spine straight and shoulders relaxed. Close your eyes if you feel comfortable doing so or keep a soft gaze. Notice the natural flow of your breath, the rise and fall of your chest or abdomen as you breathe in and out. Then, as you breathe in, silently count 1, and as you breathe out, count 2. Continue breathing and counting up to 10, then start again from 1. If your mind wanders, gently bring your focus back to counting your breaths.

After counting to 10, pause for a moment before starting the next cycle of 1 to 10. In this pause, let go of any impatience or restlessness you may feel. Embrace the stillness and observe any sensations or thoughts that arise.

2: Repeat and Expand

Continue breathing in this way for a few minutes, gradually extending the duration if you wish. If your mind becomes busy or impatient, return to counting your breaths, allowing patience to gently guide you back to the present moment.

3: Reflect

After the exercise, take a moment to reflect on the experience. Notice any changes in your state of mind or how your body feels. Embrace the sense of calm and centeredness that emerges from cultivating patience through this mindful breath exercise.

Practicing this exercise regularly will enhance your ability to stay calm and composed in challenging situations, as patience, rather than impatience, becomes your natural response to life's ups and downs. It's also a great way to deal with restless thoughts and feelings, allowing them to flow through you so you can proceed with grace.

Learning to use the 12 powers is a continuous process. This is another way of being. Embrace the journey and the learning experiences it brings, allowing yourself to grow and flourish in harmony with your authentic self. By consistently practicing self-reflection, self-expression, and self-acceptance, you can cultivate the courage and confidence to shine brightly as your true self in all areas of life.

Remember, as Brendon Burchard says:[8]

First, it's an **intention**.

Then a **behavior**.

Then a **habit.**

Then a **practice.**

Then a **second nature.**

Then it's simply **who you are**.

In Step 2 we talked about the Hierarchy of Needs. Doing all this work is valuable, but we also need to take the time to check in with ourselves and see how we're doing when it comes to our basic foundations. While much of HFA takes place in the mind, it can also manifest in the physical world, so making sure we have enough rest and are sufficiently hydrated are also important parts of the process. It's time to take care of yourself, inside and out.

STEP 5 SUMMARY

We've looked at the 12 powers – the final pieces of the jigsaw. You may choose to use none of them, one, or all of them. Your path is your own to tread, and what works for another person may not work for you. However, kindness, self-compassion, and embracing truth are universal concepts that bring richness and depth to everyone's life. I hope you're finding your way to that space now.

Conclusion

You've made it! You started your journey in a place where, perhaps, you knew something wasn't right, but you weren't sure exactly what. Throughout this book I've challenged you to deep dive into your HFA by going to the very heart of your being – to face your core beliefs and the lies and stories you tell yourself, and confront the elephant in the room: your fear.

You bravely recognized your patterns of behavior and explored your early life experiences, seeing how they impact the person you are now. I've also shared my journey with you – the low points and the triumphs – and today I'm writing this book from a place of joy and self-compassion.

I trust that you understand yourself better now and will embrace the unique and extraordinary individual that you are, including the traits attributed to high-functioning anxiety. I've given you the tools you need to break free of the patterns and beliefs that are holding you back, and to be kind to yourself.

Your wings are ready to unfold now. It's time to soar and transcend the limitations imposed by HFA, finding empowerment through the lessons of this journey. Embrace this newfound freedom, for your journey toward self-discovery and healing has begun.

Your Contract with Self

Now that I've finished this book, I will honor a contract with myself:

I'm here to explore my inner world and understand myself better.

At times, this may not be easy and I'm aware of this. But I'm ready and empowered to learn to navigate my emotions to feel happier, more at peace, and less anxious.

I'm no longer available for things that make me feel bad about myself.

I'm showing up as me.

Signed:

Date:

Acknowledgments

I extend my heartfelt gratitude to everyone who played a pivotal role in bringing this book to life. To my family, both biological and those who have become family in the journey of life, your unwavering support and encouragement have been my anchor.

A special acknowledgment to my therapist, for her expertise and guidance, and for providing a space where I could cease dimming my light and wholeheartedly embrace it. Though it took several sessions for me to test and build my trust with her, I'm truly grateful for her not giving up on me.

To those who believed in me and illuminated my path during moments of darkness, thank you for showing me that I can trust my wings, not just to fly but to thrive. To those who have been lessons and fountains of wisdom in my life, your impact is beyond measure.

This book stands as a testament to the collective effort and shared experiences that have sculpted my journey. I express my gratitude to each of you for being an integral part of this meaningful endeavor.

References

INTRODUCTION

1. National Institute of Mental Health (NIMH), The National Institute of Mental Health Information Resource Center. Any Anxiety Disorder. www.nimh.nih.gov/health/statistics/any-anxiety-disorder [Accessed 20 November 2023]

2. Office for National Statistics (2023), 'Public opinions and social trends, Great Britain: personal well-being and loneliness.' www.ons.gov.uk/peoplepopulationandcommunity/wellbeing/datasets/publicopinionsandsocialtrendsgreatbritainpersonalwellbeingandloneliness [Accessed 20 November 2023]

STEP 2

3. Bowlby, J. (1958), 'The nature of the child's tie to his mother', *International Journal of Psycho-Analysis*, 39: 350–373.

4. Maslow, A.H. (1973), 'A theory of human motivation', in R.J. Lowry (ed.), *Dominance, self-esteem, and self-actualization: Germinal papers of H.A. Maslow*. Belmont, CA: Wadsworth, pp. 153–173.

5. Maslow, A.H. (1973), 'A theory of human motivation', in R.J. Lowry (ed.), *Dominance, self-esteem, and self-actualization: Germinal papers of H.A. Maslow*. Belmont, CA: Wadsworth, pp. 153–173.

STEP 4

6. Linden, M. and Rutkowski, K. (2013), *Hurting Memories and Beneficial Forgetting*. Amsterdam: Elsevier.

STEP 5

7. Brown, B. (2015), *Daring Greatly: How the Courage to be Vulnerable Transforms the Way We Live, Love, Parent, and Lead*. London: Penguin Books.

8. Burchard, B. (2021), @BrendonBurchard www.twitter.com/ BrendonBurchard/status/1401693297010266112?lang=en [Accessed 29 November 2023]

Index

About the Author

Dr. Lalitaa Suglani is an award-winning psychologist, renowned leadership coach, and international speaker. She has over 17 years' experience working across various clinical areas within the public and private health sector.

Lalitaa believes that the key to achieving real, lasting success and happiness in all areas of our lives lies within our own mind. She has seen how, through personal growth and self-awareness, we can learn to harness our thought patterns, gain control of the voice in our head, cultivate a positive mindset, and create the life and career of our dreams.

 www.drlalitaa.com

 @drlalitaas

 @dr.lalitaa

 @DrLalitaa

 @dr.lalitaa.psychologist

We hope you enjoyed this Hay House book. If you'd like to receive our online catalog featuring additional information on Hay House books and products, or if you'd like to find out more about the Hay Foundation, please contact:

Hay House LLC, P.O. Box 5100, Carlsbad, CA 92018-5100
(760) 431-7695 or (800) 654-5126
www.hayhouse.com® • www.hayfoundation.org

———

Published in Australia by:
Hay House Australia Publishing Pty Ltd
18/36 Ralph St., Alexandria NSW 2015
Phone: +61 (02) 9669 4299
www.hayhouse.com.au

Published in the United Kingdom by:
Hay House UK Ltd
The Sixth Floor, Watson House,
54 Baker Street, London W1U 7BU
Phone: +44 (0) 203 927 7290
www.hayhouse.co.uk

Published in India by:
Hay House Publishers (India) Pvt Ltd
Muskaan Complex, Plot No. 3,
B-2, Vasant Kunj, New Delhi 110 070
Phone: +91 11 41761620
www.hayhouse.co.in

———

Access New Knowledge.
Anytime. Anywhere.

Learn and evolve at your own pace
with the world's leading experts.

www.hayhouseU.com

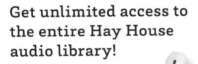

CONNECT WITH
HAY HOUSE
ONLINE

🌐 hayhouse.co.uk   **f** @hayhouse

📷 @hayhouseuk   **X** @hayhouseuk

▶ @hayhouseuk   ♪ @hayhouseuk

Find out all about our latest books & card decks • Be the first to know about exclusive discounts • Interact with our authors in live broadcasts • Celebrate the cycle of the seasons with us • Watch free videos from your favourite authors • Connect with like-minded souls

'*The gateways to wisdom and knowledge are always open.*'

Louise Hay